AF480277

CARDINAL VIRTUES
Illustrated Sayings for a Fulfilling Life

ARTURO JOSÉ SÁNCHEZ HERNÁNDEZ

2024

DEDICATION

To the warrior within us all.

TABLE OF CONTENTS

PREFACE TO THE FIRST ENGLISH EDITION

Dear reader,

It is a great pleasure to present this work in English for the first time, opening the doors to a new audience and offering the opportunity to explore a unique combination of ancient wisdom and modern technology. This book, which has been warmly received in its original Spanish edition, is now being offered to English-speaking readers with the aim of enriching their understanding of the cardinal virtues and providing valuable tools for facing the challenges of daily life.

The approach of this book is simple yet profound: to use old proverbs, distilled from centuries of human experience, and fuse them with AI-generated images. This fusion not only enhances the beauty and meaning of the proverbs but also facilitates their understanding and application in everyday life.

In this edition, the chapters explore the four cardinal virtues: prudence, justice, fortitude, and moderation. These virtues are approached from the perspective of the golden mean, an essential balance between the extremes of excess and deficiency. Additionally, the components of fortitude—courage, patience, perseverance, equanimity, and resignation—are explored in depth, highlighting how each virtue intertwines and supports the others.

This book is the result of more than thirty years of clinical observation, ethical reflection, and commitment to mental health and well-being. In adapting it to English, I hope that the lessons contained here resonate with the same clarity and strength as in its original language, helping more people to live with greater wisdom and balance.

I invite you to immerse yourself in this work, which not only offers an ethical guide but also a constant source of inspiration, now accessible to a broader audience. May these pages serve as a beacon on your path to personal excellence.

With gratitude and anticipation,

Arturo José Sánchez Hernández

~~~

PREFACE TO THE SECOND SPANISH EDITION

Dear reader, in this book you are about to dive into, the ancient wisdom of old proverbs intertwines with AI-generated images, offering a unique resource to navigate the complexities of daily life, make wise decisions, and live a full and meaningful life. By merging these images with the proverbs, we embark on a journey through the cardinal virtues: prudence, justice, fortitude, and moderation, approached from the philosophy of the golden mean. This philosophy teaches us that these virtues are found in a balance between two vicious extremes: excess and deficiency. The proverbs and images aim to capture the essence of this ethical equilibrium.

The first four chapters of the book are dedicated to exploring each of the cardinal virtues, while the following five chapters focus on breaking down the components of fortitude: courage, patience, perseverance, equanimity, and resignation. The tenth chapter highlights the interconnection and importance of each cardinal virtue for the flourishing of the others. Additionally, several glossaries are included that delve into the theory of virtue and the terms associated with each examined quality.

Each chapter is accompanied by a summary that distills its essence, and at the conclusion of the book, you will find "General Considerations on the Cardinal Virtues." This segment presents, concisely, the central ideas of the book, beginning with an inspiring exhortation, followed by a brief explanation, and culminating with the timeless wisdom of a proverb.

It is noteworthy that this project constitutes a mature work, forged over more than thirty years of clinical observation, compassionate listening, and narrative reflection by the author, who brings experience as a doctor, writer, psychiatrist, sexologist, and psychotherapist.

I invite you to immerse yourself in this harmonious dialogue, where proverbs and images, intertwined, narrate the eternal story of human excellence. May this journey inspire your life in harmony with the virtues that have guided humanity through the ages.

The Author.

~~~

PROLOGUE TO THE FIRST SPANISH EDITION

We are presented with an original book written by a young and equally original talent. In the following pages, the reader will find wisdom and enjoy a journey through images, maxims, proverbs, and sayings, all connected by the thread of the message the author seeks to convey through a work rich in teachings: the value of cardinal virtues for the balance of personality and the flourishing of mental and spiritual health.

It addresses philosophy and ethics, complex topics, in an engaging and comprehensible manner. It gently leads us to reason, directly engaging our right hemisphere, which deals with our higher mental syntheses, without the dense circumlocutions typical of the formal logical approach's slow passage through the left hemisphere.

Arturo Sánchez is a psychiatrist deeply immersed in Philosophy and, at the same time, a philosopher enamored with the Psychiatry he practices. He is also a writer and illustrator, a scientist, and a farmer; above all, a modest and simple man. I stated at the outset that he is an original individual with an original work that I recommend reading: you will not regret it. Being young, he still has much creative work ahead of him. We will hear more about him in the future, as he has much to contribute to Psychiatry and Cuban Social Sciences.

In this, his literary "opus prima," the reader will learn. I learned, even though I am much older than him. It is worth noting that Dr. Sánchez, a specialist in Comprehensive General Medicine with honors, an internationalist, before completing his second specialization in Psychiatry while diligently fulfilling his duties and multiple tasks as a resident, was already a Master of Science and had his thesis ready for a Doctorate in Philosophical Sciences. Is any further recommendation needed?

If, as his tutor and friend, I suffer from catatimia, you will decide.

Dr.C Alberto Clavijo Portieles
Vice President of the Cuban Society of Psychiatry
Camagüey, Cuba
December 2010

~~~

INTRODUCTION

To understand the importance of the cardinal virtues: prudence, moderation, justice, and fortitude, it is necessary first to define what we mean by virtue and its opposite, vice.

The word "virtue" derives from the Latin "virtus," and like its Greek equivalent "areté," it refers to the excellent quality of something or someone in fulfilling their functions. For example, the "areté" of a knife is manifested in its sharpness, ease of handling, lightness, among other qualities. In the case of people, talking about virtue or "areté" implies referring to the qualities that allow them to excel in various areas, such as art, sports, or science. Specifically, moral virtue or "êthiké areté" refers to the excellent qualities of a person in the moral realm.[1]

On the other hand, the term "vice" denotes the poor quality of something or someone in performing their functions. A vice in a knife could be its lack of sharpness, discomfort in use, or excessive weight. In the moral realm, a vice represents a negative quality in a person that hinders or complicates their ability to fulfill their roles within society, thus affecting the performance of their functions.[2]

Moral virtues, understood as positive moral qualities, manifest in mature thoughts, feelings, and actions that generate the best outcomes both for those who act and for those impacted by those actions. These virtues are crucial for maintaining proper relationships with others, with oneself, and with the environment, and for effectively facing both the extraordinary but infrequent demands of life and the ordinary but everyday challenges.

The cardinal virtues form the foundation of all other moral qualities, highlighting their transcendent importance. Distortions of these virtues lead to deficiencies in many other virtues. For example, alterations in fortitude can result in weakness or rigidity, cowardice or recklessness, inconsistency or obstinacy, impatience or passivity. These deviations can, in turn, complicate the ability to be just, as defending principles requires courage. This impairment of justice will then be reflected in a broad spectrum of negative moral qualities.

Furthermore, because the impact of the cardinal virtues on other moral qualities is very significant, sustained alterations in these can manifest as chronic suffering, even when all necessary conditions for living fully are present. Such a situation is incompatible with good mental health and often affects biological health as well. This type of longterm deficiency could be considered a form of insufficiency, not cardiac or renal, but rather existential.

The theoretical treatment of the cardinal virtues dates back to antiquity, specifically in what is known as Virtue Theory or Aretology. Socrates (470399 B.C.), one of the first thinkers to address this topic, argued that happiness or eudaimonia represents the highest good and linked virtue to knowledge.[3] According to this view, those who know what is good also practice it, an idea described as intellectualism or ethical rationalism.

By emphasizing reason as the guide for action and the foundation of moral virtues, ethical rationalism underscores individual responsibility in decision-making, which is a very positive aspect. However, knowledge alone is not the only determinant of behavior, nor does it ensure that one acts correctly. If the individual is not emotionally motivated, behavior does not change. If it were otherwise, therapies for treating addictions like alcoholism or smoking would be reduced to educational talks or recommended readings, which is evidently insufficient.

For Aristippus of Cyrene (435354 B.C.) and his followers, known as the Cyrenaics, the purpose and highest good of human life lies in the pursuit of the greatest possible pleasure; this philosophy is known as hedonism. The Cyrenaics gave preference to sensual pleasures over intellectual ones. However, Aristippus emphasized that humans should not become slaves to their pleasures but aspire to prudent and moderate enjoyment.

Hedonism emphasizes the importance of living in the moment and enjoying life's pleasures here and now. This perspective can help people value the present and find joy in everyday experiences. However, the constant pursuit of pleasure can result in unsustainable behaviors in the long term, particularly those related to addictions. Moreover, by exclusively prioritizing pleasure, hedonism can devalue effort, sacrifice, and facing challenges, which are essential for personal and moral growth.

The Cynics, including Antisthenes (444369 B.C.) and Diogenes of Sinope (414324 B.C.), adopted a stance contrary to the Cyrenaic hedonism. They argued that the essence of virtue lies in self-control and the disdain for pleasure, which they considered an evil to be avoided.

These thinkers held that the goal of a virtuous life is achieved through the tranquility obtained by renouncing everything that makes man dependent, including material goods, pleasures, and social norms. They advocated for disdain towards satisfying nonessential needs and mocked conventionalism, often challenging and violating established standards of decorum.[4]

Cynicism values self-control and independence, aspects that can be considered positive, but its focus on renunciation can limit the development of other virtues and personal skills that require interaction and engagement with society. Given the Cynics' disdain for conventionalism and decorum, their positions can conflict with community values and norms, leading to tensions and difficulties in social and professional relationships.

Plato (427347 B.C.) distinguished himself from Socrates by arguing that virtue is not merely reduced to knowledge but also includes wisdom, justice, temperance, and fortitude. According to him, these qualities are essential for achieving proper harmony in human activity, which is assumed in the present study.

Notable aspects of this thinker include his conception of the good as an essential element of reality, and that evil does not exist in itself but is an imperfect reflection of the good. He also proposed that the highest good consists of a perfect imitation of God. This perspective can be considered disconnected from the practical and everyday realities of human life, making it difficult to apply in concrete situations.

Aristotle (384322 B.C.), like Plato, maintained that virtue transcends mere knowledge. He considered justice as a "compendium" of all other virtues. He proposed that moral virtues are habits of choice or volitional preferences that make a man good and the work he does good.[5] These virtues constitute intermediate positions between vicious extremes, one by excess and the other by deficiency.[6] Despite this, they are not a tendency toward mediocrity; from the perspective of perfection and good, they constitute a "pinnacle or extreme."

He also argued that moral virtues can only be acquired through the repetition and correction of actions and always occur in relationships between human beings. For this thinker, the moral evaluation of an act presupposes the attribution of responsibility to the moral agent, and responsibility implies voluntariness.[7] Aristotle also emphasized the circumstantial nature of virtue, explaining that virtues are about acting how, when, where, and in the manner that is appropriate.[8]

The fundamental orientation of his ethical philosophical system is happiness (eudaimonism). Regarding the virtue between vicious extremes, Aristotle argued that such a conception is not applicable to justice.[9] In this work, moderation and prudence are also excluded from this conception for the same reasons Aristotle gives for justice; each has only one vicious extreme: injustice, immoderation, and imprudence, respectively. However, there are particular forms of these unique extremes, which arise from the existence of some vice for which both extremes exist. Of the qualities discussed in this work, this conception applies only to fortitude and its components: courage, patience, perseverance, equanimity, and resignation.

For the Stoics, virtue consists in the elimination of all passions and the acceptance of the order of nature, which is orderly and rational. Only a life in harmony with this can be good. They advocated for independence from material circumstances and maintained that passions and affections are bad, so the wise man is independent of these.[10]

However, it is important to note that passions and affections are inseparable components of human nature. While it is crucial for humans to educate themselves in the most mature ways of feeling and reacting to reality, affectivity is an essential link between our needs and the environment, which, to a greater or lesser extent, offers the necessary elements for their satisfaction.

In the Middle Ages, Ambrose of Milan (339397)[11] is credited with introducing the notion of cardinal virtues, which refer to the moral qualities discussed in this work: prudence, fortitude, justice, and moderation.[12]

Thomas Aquinas (12251274) reconciled Aristotelianism with the authority of the Church. He accepted the treatment of virtues by Plato and Aristotle, considering that prudence, justice, fortitude, and temperance constitute the foundation of all others. According to this thinker, these "type virtues" perfectly realize the four general modes of virtue: rational determination of the good (prudence), establishment of the good (justice), firmness to adhere to the good (fortitude), and moderation to avoid being drawn to evil (temperance).[13] He emphasized the socalled theological virtues: faith, hope, and charity, which he defined as habits infused by God. The fundamental orientation of his doctrine is God.

In the present work, the fundamental orientation is happiness, aligning with the eudaimonic proposal of Socrates and Aristotle. Similarly, it agrees with the view that the qualities of prudence, justice, fortitude, and moderation are the foundation or principle of all others, thus deserving the designation of cardinal virtues.

Since the Renaissance, virtue theory, which had the cardinal virtues at its core, ceased to be the predominant ethical conception. However, these qualities have continued to be addressed, mainly from the perspectives of Ethics and Axiology or the Theory of Values.[14] Often, though, they are treated in isolation, disregarding the link between them and their impact on other moral qualities.

This research aims to delve deeper into the study of the cardinal virtues and contribute to their dissemination. To achieve this, it addresses the following questions: What does each cardinal virtue consist of? What are their vicious extremes? What links exist between them? And how can understanding them be enhanced through the use of proverbs and images? The answer to this last question is mainly practical.

Proverbs and sayings have been employed that are sometimes quite similar, which is not out of fear of being misunderstood, as each group of them is accompanied by a prior explanation. This has been done so that the reader can choose the one that best suits their lexicon and way of reasoning. Because proverbs encapsulate general principles of behavior or interpretation of reality, and given their high level of synthesis and simplicity, they are easier to use in decision-making than the detailed explanations that precede them.

As bibliographic sources, classical authors in ethics such as Aristotle, Plato, Seneca, and Socrates were consulted, as well as recent researchers in the field of value theory like José Ramón Fabelo Corzo and Fernando González Rey. Additionally, there have been influences from the Argentine Risieri Frondizi.

Regarding the proverbs, maxims, and sayings, an intensive search was conducted in texts from different religions such as the Bible, the Tao Te Ching, the Analects of Confucius, encyclopedias, and dictionaries of quotes and famous phrases, as well as works by the researcher Samuel Feijóo. It should be noted that no source was discarded in the selection of proverbs and sayings. In fact, many were directly collected from popular wisdom, captured in everyday moments.

The quotes from Napoleon Bonaparte are extracted from "The Prince" by Niccolò Machiavelli, published in 1955 by Editorial Sopena of Argentina, which includes notes supposedly made by him in a copy of that volume.[15] The editors of that 1955 version assume that such notes constitute an ingenious set of ideas that Napoleon expressed or might have expressed at various times during his tumultuous public life. Therefore, while they accept that these notes may be his, they do not assume that he wrote them in a copy of "The Prince." In any case, these notes help enrich the subject matter, regardless of their authorship or whether they were written by him in that work.

The images were created using DALLE 3 artificial intelligence from Chat GPT Plus, according to the objectives of the work.

This book can serve as an auxiliary text for all those who, in their professional endeavors, cultivate moral qualities and also for researchers and those interested in the subject matter. For those practicing psychotherapy, it may be of interest due to the guiding and inspiring reflections presented, some of which have their source in the author's own professional activity as a psychotherapist.

Once the reader is presented with the historical background of the topic addressed, the positions and sources assumed by the author, and what they will find in this text, it is now fully at their disposal.

~≈~

Chapter 1. PRUDENCE

If you do not know where you are going, there will be
no path to take you there. (Quran) [16]

Prudence is a form of practical or action oriented wisdom that enables one to make decisions and manage their life properly, as well as to act and speak with wit and timeliness.[17] Its components include:

1. The ability to guide life towards good ends or objectives through good means.

2. The discernment of what is good or bad, to follow the good and avoid the bad, as the case may be.[18]

3. The skill to deliberate adequately and make sound decisions, especially in difficult situations.

Ability to Guide Life Towards Good Ends or Objectives Through Good Means

Objectives are the mental anticipation of an outcome towards which activity is directed. They function as a standard by which an individual selfregulates their behavior, comparing them with the current situation and, based on that comparison, evaluating and correcting the means and procedures employed.

There are different levels of generalization of objectives. A goal can be a specific objective of a more general one, which in turn can be specific to an even more general objective. The more general a goal, the more meaning it provides to an individual's behavior, but it offers fewer details on how to achieve it, which is provided by those with a lower degree of generalization. For example, completing a university degree, which is achieved over several years, is reached through a hierarchy of objectives, where the less general ones must be translated into daily or almost daily activities aimed at achieving it.

Knowing the more general objectives helps to understand the importance of achieving the particular objectives. This also enhances the ability to improvise and prevents confusion and errors in prioritization. When one knows the specific objectives, their behavior will be more effective in reaching the general objective.

- *When general principles are determined beforehand, there will be no confusion at the moment of action. (Confucius)[19]*
- *If you know what you want, you can make mistakes like everyone else, but you will make fewer mistakes.*

Objectives are focal points for our will and energy.

Without knowledge of particular objectives, one will be lost in relation to the general objective to which they contribute. If there is no sense of life as a system of objectives that justify an individual's existence in their own eyes, they will be lost in relation to themselves and their own existence, which is incompatible with mental health.

—To beautify life is to give it purpose. (José Martí)[20]

—Only after having a defined purpose in life can we achieve peace of mind. Only after achieving peace of mind can we enjoy peaceful rest. (Confucius)[21]

Quality of Objectives

To say that an individual is prudent, it is not enough for them to have objectives and know which means to use to achieve them. It is important that these objectives are correct from an ethical-moral standpoint.

For the most general ends towards which life is oriented to be correct from an ethical-moral perspective, they must have the following characteristics:

—Be achievable.

—Be an expression of our true self.

—Have a projection towards others and bring benefit to society.

—The activity through which these objectives are expressed should not cause unjustified imbalances in the individual pursuing them, nor in others.

Objectives must be achievable; otherwise, they constitute a form of disorientation. There are no effective means or procedures to achieve unattainable goals, as they cannot be realized because the means available to or potentially available to the individual are insufficient and ineffective.

—An unattainable goal signifies failure from its very conception.

The presence of unattainable goals is a form of disorientation that leads to wasted time, resources, and valuable opportunities to achieve other, more realistic goals. This guarantees feeling frustrated and stuck in the same place.

—He who strives to make an impossible dream come true fails. (Afro-Cuban saying)[22]

—If you know you won't reach the goal, don't start.

—It is not wise to pursue what does not promise success. (Afro-Cuban saying)[23]

Goals that are not achievable today may become so tomorrow, and vice versa; those that are perfectly achievable today may cease to be so tomorrow. At this point in the analysis, it is important to differentiate between unattainable goals and difficult but possible ones.

—Difficult does not mean impossible.

Many times, a difficult goal seems impossible to most people, but not to the one who fights for it and conquers it, even despite the opinions of others who tried to discourage them.

When someone tells you that you can't, they are often speaking of their own limitations, not yours.

—Man disapproves of what he cannot achieve. (Afro-Cuban saying) [24]

And it is through the perfection and greatness of the goal once projected that the perfection and greatness of what is conquered are achieved.

—The perfection of the form is almost always achieved at the expense of the perfection of the idea. (José Martí) [25]

—If you want to be Pope, set it in your mind.

—He who aspires to be an eagle must fly high and look far.

—To be great, think big and attempt great things.

An individual's most important goals must be a genuine expression of their being, ensuring real motivation and commitment to achieve them. Often, what is interpreted as a lack of willpower is actually a weakness in the motives related to the proposed objectives.

—Weakness of will or weakness of objectives?

They must have a projection towards others and bring benefit to society: the efforts made to achieve them should contribute to the development and self-realization of other people, generating a sense of usefulness and contributing to personal happiness.

—In seeking joys, I found that life was service; I served and found that service was joy. [26]

—Let each man learn to do something that others need. (José Martí) [27]

—In seeking the good of others, we find our own.

—The path to happiness lies in serving others.

A negative version of the previous statement would be: The most significant personal objectives that do not positively contribute or that have an unjustified negative impact on the development of others are questionable from an ethical-moral standpoint.

—If you cannot do good, at least do no harm.

Similarly, the activities through which objectives are pursued should not cause unjustified imbalances in the person seeking to achieve them. This often happens with various vices that, although they may seem attractive and offer temporary pleasure, have harmful consequences.

—Vice is a precipice. (Cuba) [28]

−Vice crafts its own torment with its hands.

−There is no vice without torment. (Spain)[29]

−There are paths that seem right, but in the end, they lead to death. (Proverbs 14:1216:25)[30]

The intensity with which a person pursues their goals should not cause them harm. This is evident in cases such as work addiction, where, despite significantly contributing to the wellbeing of others, it causes an unjustified imbalance in those who suffer from it. This happens because, by excessively prioritizing certain work or domestic responsibilities, other important aspects of life are neglected, resulting in exhaustion, decreased performance, and deterioration of health, which can have severe consequences.[31]

−A fertile field, if not allowed to rest, becomes barren. (Spain)[32]

−The string, if too tight, snaps. (San Salvador)[33]

−Too much running results in little progress. (Spain)[34]

−Too much stretching causes breaking. (Spain)[35]

−He who runs much, soon stops. (Spain)[36]

To achieve any objective, means are necessary. It should be noted that although a particular objective can be considered a means to achieve more generalized objectives, the concept of means is much broader: it consists of anything that can serve the achievement of a specific end. Therefore, in addition to particular objectives, it includes procedures as well as any type of material or human resource.

There is a close relationship between objectives and means. Without objectives, the means are meaningless, and without adequate means, the objectives cannot be achieved.

−Ends without means are empty, and means without ends are blind.

Quality of Means

With one egg, you will not break the rock.
(Czechoslovakia)[37]

Prudence also includes choosing good means, which must have a set of characteristics. First and foremost, they must be effective, meaning they truly have the potential to lead the user to the achievement of their goals. Otherwise, they will only bring failure.

−*A gourd with a hole is useless as a cup. (Cuba)*[38]

−*A chair without a seat is useless for sitting. (Afro-Cuban saying)*[39]

−*A lamp without a wick, what good is it?*

If you are looking for fish, don't climb a tree. (China)[40]

This is valid for both the resources used and the procedures developed.

−A shout doesn't kill a rabbit, even if wellaimed.

−You can't fill your belly by painting bread. (China)[41]

Secondly, they should enable the achievement of objectives with a positive or acceptable cost-benefit ratio, which is efficiency. Otherwise, one might incur a Pyrrhic victory, where the cost is excessively high.

−If I lose more than I gain, what do I gain?

−Another victory like this, and I'm lost.

−The broth ended up costing more than the meatballs. (Mexico)[42]

However, efficacy and efficiency are not, and cannot be, the only criteria for the quality of means. They must be chosen within the framework of respecting others' rights and one's own.

−Do not seek good ends by vile means.

−Pursue the best ends with the best means.

Moreover, the pursuit of ethically correct means should not degenerate into unnecessary and paralyzing considerations. It is important to differentiate between means that are ethically and morally incorrect and those that, while having nothing negative against them in that sense, are difficult to use because they are different from or contrary to what one is accustomed to.

Sometimes, they are the best option, and although it may be unpleasant or painful to use them, it is worse not to do so.

—*Do not show deference to others to your own detriment, and do not be ashamed to your own ruin. (Ecclesiasticus 4:22)*[43]

—*A merciful surgeon never made a good cure.*

—*You have to break the egg before making the omelet. (Mexico)*[44]

—*There is no omelet without breaking eggs. (Mexico)*[45]

—*There are painful procedures that are inevitable and even necessary.*

—*Better to turn green once than yellow a hundred times. (Spain)*[46]

Discernment of What is Good and Desirable from What is Bad and Avoidable

To bread, bread and wine, wine. (Spain)[47]

Another component of prudence is discernment. To discern means to distinguish something from another, highlighting the difference between them.

—*Call a spade a spade.*

—*Things by their proper names.*

In the case of prudence, this quality refers to the ability to distinguish between what is good and therefore desirable, and what is bad and should be avoided.

- *"Prudence is knowing how to distinguish things that can be desired from those that should be avoided." (Cicero)*[48]

Discernment involves looking beyond the outward appearance of things.

- *Appearances can be deceiving.*

- *Look closely; what seems may not be, and what is may surprise you. (Afro-Cuban saying)*[49]

- *Do not judge the tree by its bark.*

- *Not everything that glitters is gold; nor is gold always visible, even if it is right in front of us.*

Under the sheep's skin, the wolf's intention often hides.[50]

And this is especially important when identifying the false appearance of security that circumstances can have.

- *Underneath trust, danger sleeps. (Cuba)*[51]

- *Don't think that because the water is calm there are no crocodiles in it.*

- *Not all closed eyes are sleeping. (United States)*[52]

−Some have sweet words in their mouth and a knife in their heart. (India)[53]
−Faces we see, hearts we don't know. (Mexico)[54]

Thieves pray for there to be trusting and sleepy
people.

Discernment allows us to distinguish the trustworthy from the untrustworthy, which is an important step in correctly placing caution and trust.

−The harm that arises from trust uproots you completely. (Panchatantra)[55]

−Unexpected misfortune strikes us more severely.

Ability to Deliberate and Decide Adequately, Especially in Difficult Situations

The last component of prudence to analyze is the ability to deliberate and decide adequately, especially in difficult situations.

Deliberation involves resolving something with forethought. This quality allows for careful and thorough consideration of the pros and cons of the reasons for a decision before making it, and the rightness or wrongness of choices before expressing them.

The dog has four legs but can only take one path.
(Afro-Cuban saying)[56]

Deciding is the process by which an individual chooses between two or more possible alternatives, for which they must form a definitive judgment about something that was uncertain and determine their course of action. Decision-making begins with deliberation and ends in action; without action, the process remains incomplete.

—Ideas are useless if you don't put them into action.

—Bring your ideas to action so they aren't just an illusion.

—Take time to deliberate, but when the time to act comes, stop thinking and act.

—Sometimes we have everything we need to move forward; we just need to take action.

Through decision-making, an individual chooses between possible options, many of which frequently exclude others.

—You can't blow and sip at the same time. (Spain)[57]

—You can't ring the bells and be in the procession. (Spain)[58]

Something that plays an essential role in decision-making is the will, which allows for the selection, prioritization, and activation of some motives in relation to others, which are weakened or inhibited. This is done based on some goal or ideal. With a strong will, there will be firmness in decisions.

−The root of decisions is the will. (Ecclesiasticus 37:17)[59]

−The will creates paths. (Germany)[60]

−There is a driving force more powerful than steam and electricity: the will. (José de la Luz y Caballero)[61]

−The strong willed swim across the sea of life, while the weak only bathe in it.

Making a decision involves choosing to act or not, waiting for more favorable conditions to intervene or acquiring more information before deliberating, or allowing others to make the decision. However, beyond what is chosen, decisions define the moral development of the individual.

−A man is measured by the quality of his decisions.

It's not about only making the right decisions to succeed in an endeavor or in life. Success is built with both successes and mistakes. Every decision has a margin of error, and making mistakes is part of existence, so we should not fear honest errors.

−Mistakes are the portals of discovery.

−Failure is not falling down but refusing to get up.

−The road to triumph is paved with good and bad decisions.[62]

−Error is essential on the path to learning.

−Stumbling is how one learns to walk.

Often, indecision is much more harmful than the least good of the decisions we might make.

−Decisions can be good or bad, but what always has been, is, and will be bad is indecision.[63]

−Much hesitation, little success.

−He who hesitates too much in choosing, ends up with the worst.

−Opportunity is sometimes lost in deliberations.

On the other hand, the indecisive person keeps postponing necessary decisions, and their problems accumulate.

−He who postpones his resolutions from one day to the next always lives overwhelmed by troubles. (Hesiod)[64]

Disposition to Act and Speak with Sharpness, Wit, and Opportunity

Prudence involves the ability to act or speak with tact and timeliness, thereby avoiding harmful consequences of actions or words.

—In opportunity lies triumph.

A difficult aspect of being timely is knowing when to speak and when to remain silent as circumstances require.

—The art of silence is as great as the art of speech. (Germany)[65]

—There is a time to be silent and a time to speak. (Ecclesiastes 3:7)[66]

—How good is a timely word!

—A word fitly spoken is like apples of gold in settings of silver. (Proverbs 25:11)[67]

—He who knows nothing else knows enough if he knows when to be silent. (Italy)[68]

"Oh, that I had a guard for my mouth and a seal of discretion on my lips, so that they would not cause my downfall, nor my tongue be my ruin!" (Ecclesiasticus 22:27) [69]

There is compromising information that, if revealed in certain places,[70] at certain times, or in front of certain people, can bring bad consequences, so it is important to be careful in this regard.

– *Do not speak excessively to avoid entangling and stumbling.*

– *Discretion is a weapon of protection.*

– *Speaking blindly can complicate everything; discretion is a wise method.*

– *When words are many, transgression is not lacking; but whoever restrains his lips is wise. (Proverbs 10:19)[71]*

– *He who talks too much is bound to make mistakes. (Galicia, Spain)[72]*

Release ideas, but seal your lips. (Egypt)[73]

Sometimes, revealing or making certain information evident can bring such negative consequences that it should be carefully guarded, despite how friendly others may seem or how harmless the circumstances appear.

- *Your friend has a friend, and your friend's friend has another friend; therefore, be discreet.*
- *Will you keep a secret for me, friend...? Better you keep it if I don't tell you.*
- *To keep your secret from the enemy, don't tell it to your friend. (Benjamin Franklin)[74]*
- *If you don't want a secret to be known, keep it in your knapsack. (Cuba)[75]*
- *If you don't want noise, don't drag dry leaves. (Cuba)[76]*
- *Before telling secrets on the road, check the underbrush. (China)[77]*

One must also be careful when sharing personal happiness or plans, as this can excite the self-love of others and arouse destructive envy.

- *From not keeping quiet about happiness, envy is born.*
- *Do not consult with your rivals, and hide your plans from those who are jealous of you. (Ecclesiasticus 37:10)[78]*
- *Of good things, do not speak. (Afro-Cuban saying)[79]*
- *He who won and kept quiet did what he should. (Spain)[80]*

IMPRUDENCE

A ship without a rudder is soon lost. (Spain)[81]

Imprudence is the lack of ability to make proper decisions and guide life towards good ends through good means, leading individuals to face the negative consequences of their actions.

–*He who walks badly ends badly. (Proverbs 10:9)*[82]

–*He who treads on bad paths will eventually slip. (Chile)*[83]

–*The prudent see danger and take refuge, but the simple keep going and pay the penalty. (Proverbs 22:3 and 27:12)*[84]

There are many moral vices that lead to imprudence, but two very important ones are impulsivity and indiscretion.

Impulsivity

Impulsivity is the quality of someone who tends to speak or act thoughtlessly, driven by their impulses and the impression of the moment, without considering the consequences of their actions or words.

–*Acting without thinking can make us stumble.*

–*An angry person stirs up conflict, and a hot-tempered person commits many sins. (Proverbs 29:22)*[85]

–*Don't act on the first impulse. (Cuba)*[86]

Indiscretion

The fish dies through the mouth. (Spain)[87]

Imprudence not only manifests in rash actions that can become self-destructive but also in speaking or remaining silent inopportunely and without tact, often revealing information that should be kept hidden.

–*The hen loses its nest by clucking. (Cuba)*[88]

–*The milkman wasn't killed for watering down the milk, but for talking about it.*

–*The fool neither knows how to speak nor to be silent. (Czechoslovakia)*[89]

–*Speaking without thinking is like shooting without aiming.*

–*Much talk leads to saying foolish things. (Ecclesiastes 5:3)*[90]

–*Better to stumble with your feet than with your tongue. (Ecclesiasticus 20:18)*[91]

Quite frequently, a secret that should have been carefully guarded is revealed in a state of intoxication.

–*In wine, there is truth. (Latin Proverb: In vino veritas)*[92]

–*The more wine enters, the more secrets come out. (Spain)*[93]

–*Where wine rules, there are no secrets.*

At other times, keeping a secret is a heavy burden for the imprudent, who find it very difficult to restrain themselves.

-*An imprudent person keeping a secret suffers more than a woman in labor. (Ecclesiasticus 19:11)*[94]

-*Like an arrow stuck in the leg is a secret in the heart of an imprudent person. (Ecclesiasticus 19:12)*[95]

FINAL CONSIDERATIONS

Prudence is a form of practical or action oriented wisdom that enables one to make decisions and manage one's life properly, as well as to speak and act with wit and timeliness. Its components include:

Ability to Guide Life Towards Good Ends Through Good Means:

- *Having achievable objectives with which one is emotionally committed.*

- *Knowing how to choose the right means to achieve these objectives.*

- *Both the objectives and the means chosen should have a projection towards others and benefit society, contributing to the development and self-realization of other individuals.*

- *The activity aimed at achieving the objectives should not cause unjustified imbalances to the individual striving to reach them.*

Discernment of What is Good or Bad, to Follow or Avoid Accordingly:

- *Being able to look beyond the outward appearance of things.*

- *Knowing how to distinguish between what is good and desirable, and what is bad and avoidable, as well as what is trustworthy and what is not.*

- *Correctly placing caution and trust.*

Ability to Deliberate Adequately and Make Sound Decisions, especially in Difficult Situations: Carefully and thoroughly considering the pros and cons of the reasons for a decision before making it, and the rightness or wrongness of choices before expressing them.

Disposition to Act and Speak with Sharpness, Wit, and Opportunity: Being able to act or speak when circumstances require it, and having the ability to conceal information that should not be known by others.

~~~

Chapter 2. MODERATION

Neither so cold that it freezes, nor so hot that it burns.

Moderation is the ability to avoid both excesses and deficiencies.

–*Virtue lies in the middle. (Latin Proverb: In medio stat virtus)*[96]

–*Go in the middle and you will not fall. (Spain)*[97]

–*Between the brake and the spur, a good middle is achieved.*

–*Neither so much "giddy up" that it runs away, nor so much "whoa" that it stops. (Galicia, Spain)*[98]

–*Neither so high that it reaches the sky, nor so low that it crawls on the ground.*

–*It's just as bad to go too far as not to go far enough. (Cuba)*[99]

And since it makes it possible to maintain a middle ground between vicious extremes, moderation is the foundation of many other moral qualities.

–*Moderation is the silk thread running through the pearl chain of all virtues.*[100]

Due to this, it is essential for achieving a full and successful life.

–*For a prosperous life, art, order, and measure. (Spain)*[101]

–*Happiness springs from moderation. (Goethe)*[102]

For this quality to exist, self-restraint and the ability to self-motivated are of extraordinary importance.

Continence

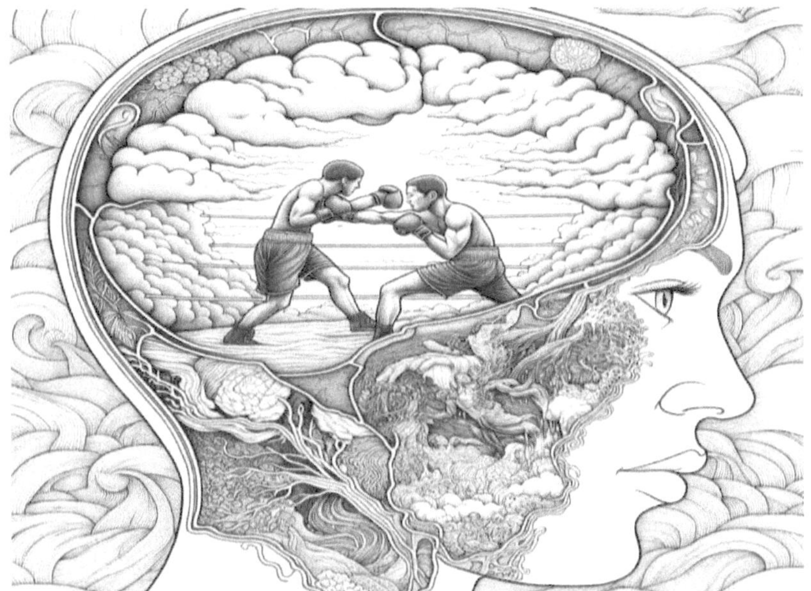

The hardest battle is the one that takes place within oneself.

Self-restraint is the ability to abstain from doing something that is intensely desired but recognized as inappropriate or harmful. In this sense, it consists of knowing how to say "No" to oneself. And this, quite often, is a very difficult battle.

- *Imposing your will on others is a demonstration of ordinary strength. Imposing it on yourself is a testimony of true power. (Lao Tzu)[103]*
- *Do not yield to unrefined desires, nor capitulate to every impulse.*
- *Do not become a slave to your desires; be worthy.*
- *I am free when, at each choice, I choose... not what pleases me most, but what makes me the best person.*

Do not be led by passion, so that it does not destroy your strength like a bull. (Ecclesiasticus 6:2)[104]

Sometimes the inappropriateness lies in the circumstances, which are not suitable for action, and this quality also allows for deferring the execution of what one desires to do until the moment is opportune.

–*The wise... in their actions, love to find the right moment. (Lao Tzu)*[105]

In the process of avoiding what one knows should not be done, it is sometimes necessary to restrain intense desires, passions, or feelings.

–*Clip the wings of your chickens and your hopes so you won't have to chase after them. (Benjamin Franklin)*[106]

–*Control your desires and emotions, or they will control you.*

–*Conquer your passions, and you will conquer the world. (India)*[107]

–*Better to conquer oneself than to capture cities. (Proverbs 16:32)*[108]

In this inner battle, the individual may be externally stimulated to do what they know they should not, which is temptation. The ability to overcome these temptations is an important indicator of a person's moral culture.

–*The ability to withstand temptations gives us the true measure of character.*

–*Opportunity makes one sin. The weak one.*

This ability to say "No" to oneself helps to avoid excesses and the harm they produce.

–Enough is better than too much.

–Knowing when it is enough, you will always have enough.

–Those who know when they have enough are rich. (China)[109]

–...He who knows when to stop does not continue towards danger, and will endure for a long time. (Lao Tzu)[110]

Ability to Activate Oneself for Unpleasant or Undesired Activities

Knowing how to contain oneself is as important as activating oneself when circumstances require it.

–...It is necessary for desires to obey reason; neither to precede it nor abandon it due to weakness or laziness. (Marcus Tullius Cicero)[111]

This enables the performance of necessary activities that one does not want to do or finds deeply unpleasant.

–You won't always be motivated, learn to be disciplined.

–When you lack motivation, let discipline be abundant.

–Discipline takes you where motivation cannot.

When there is a lack of desire to perform necessary activities, something that works quite well is simply starting to do them.

–To begin, start doing.

–The secret to getting ahead is to start.

–The first step doesn't take you where you want to go, but it gets you out of where you are.

IMMODERATION

In everything, knowing the right measure is crucial.
(Spain)[112]

Immoderation can be defined as excessive action or feeling that compromises objectives and causes unjustified and undesired harm, both to others and oneself.

- *What exceeds the limit of moderation stands on an unstable point. (Seneca)[113]*

- *He who acts without measure will inevitably end in ruin.*

- *For lack of moderation, many die; but he who controls himself lives long. (Ecclesiasticus 37:31)[114]*

Excesses never lead to anything good, and something is excessive when it causes harm or has the potential to do so.

- *Do not squeeze the orange so much that the juice turns bitter. (Colombia)[115]*

- *Do not milk the cow so much that you draw blood.*

- *He who tightens the screw too much strips the thread. (Cuba)[116]*

- *Even nectar is poison if taken in excess. (India)[117]*

Any negative moral quality involves being excessive or insufficient, and therefore immoderate. This deviation exists fundamentally as incontinence or as the inability to activate oneself.

Incontinence

The fool gives free rein to his impulses, but the wise man eventually restrains them. (Proverbs 29:11)[118]

Incontinence consists of an individual, even knowing what to avoid and how to act correctly, acting incorrectly because they are incapable of restraining their desires. This quality is a form of weakness that can bring very bad consequences.

–*... the force of passion leads a man to ruin. (Ecclesiasticus 1:22)[119]*

–*The end of passion is the beginning of repentance. (Benjamin Franklin)[120]*

–*... violent passion destroys the one who has it and makes his enemies laugh at him. (Ecclesiasticus 6:4)[121]*

–*Blind appetite. How many does it bring to ruin!*

Inability to get motivated in the absence of a desire to engage in important activities

The lying wolf catches no prey, nor does the sleeping man gain victory. (Scandinavia)[122]

The incapacity to act is expressed when, due to lack of desire or evasiveness, necessary activities are not carried out. This can lead to postponing an inevitable and necessary unpleasant moment.

–If you flee from your battles, you will end up without finding your victories.

–Avoiding problems you need to face is equivalent to missing out on the good things in life you have the potential to enjoy.

If you consistently fail to do what needs to be done, your existence may become impoverished to the point of misery.

–When it is time to plow, the lazy man does not plow; but when the harvest comes, he seeks and finds nothing. (Proverbs 20:4)[123]

–Laziness walks so slowly that poverty soon overtakes it.

–Half of poverty is laziness. (Yugoslavia)[124]

–The rewards of the lazy are three: shame, illness, and misery. (England)[125]

–Lazy hands lead to a painful life. (Czechoslovakia)[126]

FINAL CONSIDERATIONS

Moderation is the ability to avoid both excesses and deficiencies, for which Self-restraint and the ability to activate oneself are necessary.

Self-restraint is the quality that allows one to:

−Abstain from doing something intensely desired but known to be wrong.

−Defer its execution to an opportune moment when the inappropriateness lies in the circumstances.

−Restrain intense desires, passions, or feelings and face temptations.

Self-restraint is particularly important at the boundaries between what is sufficient and therefore still productive or healthy, and what is excessive and harmful or potentially harmful.

The ability to activate oneself is an effort contrary to Self-restraint in the sense that it allows one to perform activities that are undesirable or deeply unpleasant, but necessary.

~~~

Chapter 3. JUSTICE

With one arm, you can't carry two watermelons.

Justice is the quality that inclines one to give each person what they are due, both in benefits and in punishments.

—An impartial judge gives each their due. (Spain)[127]

To understand the importance of justice in our lives, we must start with the fact that human essence is only conceivable in interaction with other human beings.

—To live is to coexist.

—There is no human being without human beings.

—One man alone is not a man. (Latin proverb)[128]

—One stick alone does not make a forest. (Afro-Cuban saying)[129]

Only through the relationships we establish with others can we achieve our goals and ideals and satisfy our needs.[130]

—One hand washes the other, and both wash the face. (Spain)[131]

—One hand alone does not clap.

—One finger cannot catch a louse. (African saying)[132]

46

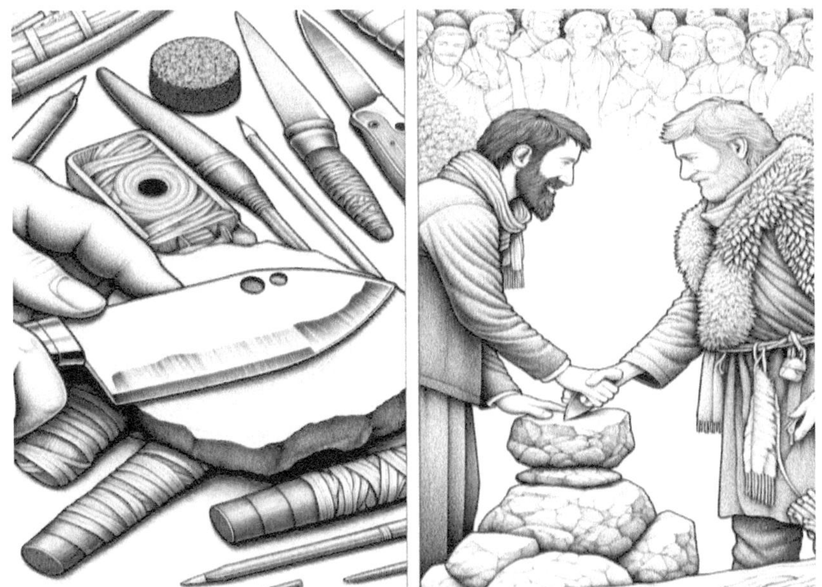

Man must sharpen himself on man as a knife on flint.
(China)[133]

And indeed, the development of our potentialities gains special momentum in our interaction with others.

—Iron sharpens iron, and one man sharpens another. (Proverbs 27:17)[134]

For relationships between human beings to be healthy, they must have order. If everyone acted without restrictions, anarchy and social indiscipline would prevail, making communal life extremely difficult. This essential social order is established through the recognition of duties and rights that regulate each individual's actions.

Duty is the moral requirement to act in a certain way, while right is the social recognition, on a moral or legal level or both, of a specific benefit or exercise of freedom.

Duties and rights are intrinsically linked. Every duty implies the rights or entitlements of other people to certain benefits, which are the result of fulfilling those duties. Similarly, rights imply duties or obligations on the part of others, whose fulfillment will result in those benefits.

—There are no rights without duties, nor duties without rights.

Justice arises from the confluence of all moral virtues but manifests clearly in a person's daily life through two of them: rectitude and assertiveness.

Rectitude

The wicked flee though no one pursues, but the righteous are as bold as a lion. (Proverbs 28:1)[135]

Rectitude is the impartiality and firmness in the resolutions taken. One of its advantages is that it allows one to sleep with a clear conscience.

–*He who does what is right, sleeps well at night.*

–*Do what you must and fear no one.*

–*He who owes nothing, fears nothing. (Proverbs 10:9)[136]*

–*If a gentleman looks within himself and is sure he has acted rightly, what has he to fear or worry about? (Confucius)[137]*

–*Resolve to act with rectitude. (Job 11:13)[138]*

Rectitude also protects against slander because, to speak ill of the righteous, one must lie, and the harmful effects of the slanderer are generally very transitory.

–*Act justly and scorn calumny; mud stains a dirty wall, but not polished marble. (Benjamin Franklin)[139]*

–*Defamation does not destroy an honest man: when the waters recede, the rock remains. (China)[140]*

–*When you do something convinced it is your duty, do not hide regardless of how unfavorable the judgment others may form of you and your actions. If the action is wrong, do not do it. If it is right, why fear those who unjustly condemn you? (Epictetus)[141]*

−*If you walk upright, there is no crooked shadow. (China)[142]*

An important indicator of an individual's moral strength is their ability to act with rectitude, even when there is no immediate and direct social pressure to do so; such as when no one is watching.

−*Laws control the lesser man; his own rectitude controls the greater one. (China)[143]*

−*The upright do what they consider right without needing an audience.*

Assertiveness

Therefore, let us be as gentle as doves and as wise as serpents.[144]

This other quality involves, first and foremost, knowing how to claim one's own rights.

−*He who exercises his right harms no one.*

It is important to consider that even if our rights have been violated, the offender also has rights that we must respect. Otherwise, we risk becoming transgressors ourselves and facing the consequences of our own excesses.

−*The faults of others do not justify our own.*

—He who has a right does not gain the right to violate another's in order to maintain his own. (José Martí)[145]

—Do not excuse your faults with those of others. (Afro-Cuban saying)[146]

Moreover, the defense of our own rights or those of others we are responsible for protecting often must be carried out under considerable pressure and with the risk of suffering harm. Therefore, it is impossible to be just without possessing courage.

—To have principles, have courage. (China)[147]

Justice and peace kiss each other.

But in addition to knowing how to claim one's own rights, another essential element of assertiveness is respecting the rights of others, which is crucial for achieving good interpersonal relationships.

—The wise neither offend nor allow themselves to be offended.

—He who has preserved his own dignity knows the value of others' and respects it. (José Martí)[148]

—This respect for the rights of others constitutes a limit to each person's freedoms.

—Your rights end where the rights of others begin.

Golden Rule of Morality

In such cases, the roles are complex and undefined, leading to poorly defined duties and rights of each individual. On what basis can one's conduct toward others be built in such circumstances?

Treat others as you would like to be treated.

In such cases, our actions can be guided by the socalled "golden rule of morality," which has a positive version: "treat others as you would like to be treated," and a negative version: "do not do to others what you would not like them to do to you."

Confucius refers to it as the rule of the square or double standard and states the following:

– *"What a man dislikes in his superiors, he should not practice in his treatment of inferiors; what he dislikes in his inferiors, he should not practice in the services he renders to his superiors; what he dislikes in those in front of him, he should not practice with those behind him; what he dislikes in those who follow him, he should not practice with those who precede him; what he dislikes in those to his right, he should not practice with those to his left; and what he dislikes in those to his left, he should not practice with those to his right. This is the principle of the square (or double standard)." (Confucius)*[149]

He also summarizes this idea as follows:

–*"Do not do to others what you do not want for yourself." (Confucius)*[150]

This idea can be seen in the New Testament of the Bible and in the Panchatantra:

–*"So in everything, do to others what you would have them do to you." (Matthew 7:12 and Luke 6:31)*[151]

–*"Listen to what virtue consists of, and meditate on it once heard: Do not do to another what you would judge as evil for yourself." (Panchatantra)*[152]

When using this principle, one takes their own feelings as a model and point of support in relationships with others, which provides a wide margin for action.

–*Man is a mirror for man. (Turkey)*[153]

INJUSTICE

This quality consists of the habitual violation of others' rights or the failure to fulfill duties. It is caused by nearly any moral vice, but two that frequently lead to injustice are leniency and harshness.

Leniency

Showing mercy to the panther is being unjust to the lambs.

Leniency is a form of passivity that consists of excessive timidity or softness when it comes to imparting justice or claiming rights.

—He who does not punish the wicked harms the good.

—He who forgives the wicked offends the good. (Spain)[154]

—He who does not punish evil commands it to be done.(Leonardo da Vinci)[155]

—The hope of forgiveness encourages the murderer and the thief.

—Easy forgiveness makes a frequent thief.

The gentle donkey is given more load.

For those who are spineless when it comes to claiming their rights, there is always someone who will abuse them.[156]

–*He who makes himself honey, gets eaten by flies. (Panama)*[157]

–*He who makes himself honey, gets eaten by ants. (Cuba)*[158]

–*He who makes himself a lamb, gets eaten by the wolf. (Italy)*[159]

–*He who makes himself into a rope, gets strung up. (Cuba)*[160]

–*Anyone will step on a dead panther's tail. (Afro-Cuban saying)*[161]

–*Everyone insults a dead tiger's mother. (Afro-Cuban saying)*[162]

–*When an elephant slips, even a frog kicks it. (India)*[163]

–*There will always be someone who abuses the unfortunate.*

–*Everyone climbs over a low wall. (Arab proverb)*[164]

The opposite happens when one knows how to properly claim their rights.

–*He is a very fierce animal; when attacked, he defends himself. (France)*[165]

–*The mare knows whom to throw, and the dead know whom to haunt.*

–*No pig scratches itself with a thorny stick. (Cuba)*[166]

–*No fly dares to approach a boiling pot. (Spain)*[167]

–*He who pokes a wasp gets stung. (Cuba)*[168]

–*Make yourself respected, and you will be respected.*

–*Humility and fierceness, all in one piece.*

To claim your rights properly, it's important that the degree of sensitivity and reactivity to others' actions be appropriate; otherwise, you may perceive offenses even in neutral gestures or actions from others.

—If you take everything personally, you will always be offended.

Often, this heightened reactivity and overactive defenses are due to unresolved internal battles over a long period.

—Those who are not at peace with themselves are at war with the entire world.

—Some people are always angry and looking for conflicts. Stay away... The battle they are fighting is not with you, but with themselves.

—Don't waste your energy fighting with those who are at war with themselves.

It's common for someone very susceptible, in defending themselves against perceived attacks, to end up creating the same antipathy and hostility they directed at others.[169]

—Treatment is a psychological boomerang.

—As is the voice, so is the echo.

—He who hurls insults should not expect praise.

—As you sow, so shall you reap.

—If you scatter thorns, don't walk barefoot.

—He who sows the wind reaps the whirlwind. (Spain)[170]

The way others project themselves towards us will be strongly influenced by how we project ourselves towards them. Therefore, if we wish to receive good treatment and good actions, we must start by treating others well and acting kindly ourselves.

—If you don't like what you're receiving, pay attention to what you're giving.

—By giving and speaking well, one wins over others. (Spain)[171]

—He who sows well, reaps well. (Spain)[172]

—Courtesy and good speech will open a hundred doors.

Inclemency

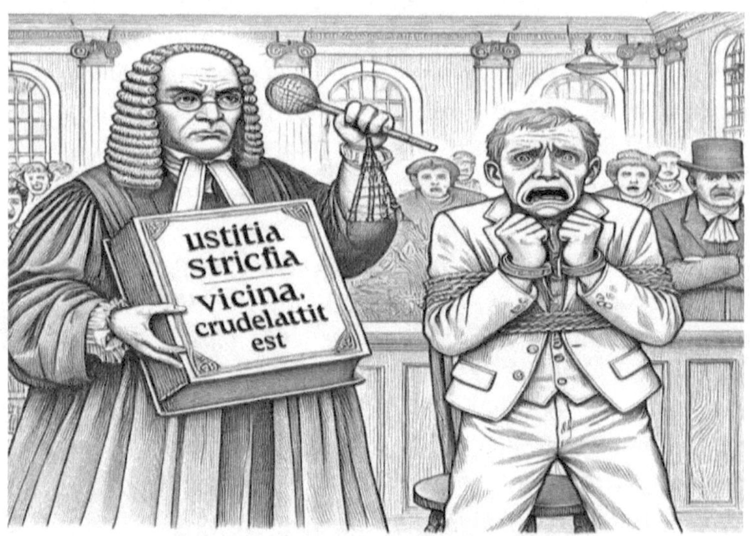

Strict justice is the neighbor of cruelty.

Harshness is the severity and rigor in the application of punishments, whether deserved or not.

–*Extreme right often becomes extreme wrong. (Spain)*[173]

–*Harshness can stem from strong feelings of insecurity that are compensated for from a position of power.*

–*The thicker the armor, the weaker the being inside.*

–*Power goes to the head when it finds an empty brain.*

FINAL CONSIDERATIONS

Justice is the quality that inclines one to give each person what they are due, both in benefits and in punishments. Among the ways justice is expressed in an individual's daily life are rectitude and assertiveness. Rectitude is the impartiality and firmness in the decisions made; assertiveness is the ability to claim one's own rights while respecting those of others.

Sometimes, the duties and rights of each person are not well defined. In these cases, our actions can be guided by the so called golden rule of morality, which has a positive version: "treat others as you would like to be treated," and a negative version: "do not do to others what you would not like done to you."

Injustice is the habitual violation of others' rights or the failure to fulfill one's duties. It is caused by any moral vice, but two that frequently lead to injustice are spinelessness and harshness. Spinelessness is excessive timidity or softness when it comes to imparting justice or claiming rights, while harshness is the severity and rigor in the application of punishments, deserved or not.

~~~

Chapter 4. STRENGTH

Straighten your heart and remain steadfast, and in times of misfortune do not be troubled. (Sirach 2:2)[174]

This quality is firmness or the ability to maintain resolutions despite internal and external pressures, in the circumstances and manner necessary to do so.

- *The best help to accomplish a project is the firmness of the person who proposes it. (Benjamin Franklin)[175]*

- *Character should be like marble: white and hard. (José Martí)[176]*

- *Blessed is the man who endures the trial with strength, for having stood the test, he will receive the crown of life. (James 1:12)[177]*

For strength to exist, it is not enough to know what must be done; it is necessary to be convinced that it is the right thing to do. It is also important that the objectives are well defined and the motivation to achieve them is strong.

- *Knowledge without heart leads nowhere.*

It is important to clarify that strength is not blind adherence to our decisions; one of its components is the ability to correct course when necessary.

- *If plan A doesn't work, remember there are other letters in the alphabet.*

- *Our heads are round to allow thoughts to change direction.*

There is no greatness without weakness.

A crucial element of strength is the recognition of one's own weaknesses, in the face of which it can be very difficult to exercise self-control. It is not about not having them, for all human beings possess them, but about the ability to identify them and take appropriate measures to overcome them or avoid falling into temptations.

−He who is unaware of his limitations overreaches and fails. (Afro-Cuban saying)[178]

Sometimes, the best way to avoid faltering in the face of our weaknesses is to stay away from what may tempt us.

−He who avoids the occasion avoids the sin.

−Want to avoid temptation? Stay away from it.

There are several qualities that constitute forms of strength, such as courage, patience, perseverance, equanimity, and resignation, which will be explained later. There are also forms of self-control, equally important, that do not have specific names, such as those exercised in the face of love, fatigue, hunger, or anger.

WEAKNESS OF THE WILL

There is no greater difficulty than a lack of will.
(Spain)[179]

At one of the vicious extremes of strength lies the weakness of will, which consists of a lack of energy in the resolutions made, making it difficult or impossible for the individual to maintain them. Even knowing how to act, they end up behaving differently.

—*The weak lack energy in their decisions.*

If the weak, with their inability to maintain resolutions and self-control as needed, end up harming themselves, how much damage can they cause to others?

—*He who trusts the weak will regret it someday.*

—*Betrayal happens more often due to weakness than a firm intention to betray.*

RIGIDITY

You won't get anywhere walking in circles.

At the other extreme of strength lies rigidity, which manifests as difficulties or inability to learn from experience and modify decisions when necessary, leading to the repetition of the same mistakes over and over again.

– *If you don't change, everything repeats.*

– *Until you change, you will continue to repeat the same experiences.*

– *Instead of asking yourself why the same things happen to you, ask yourself why you choose the same paths that lead to failure, boredom, or dissatisfaction.*

– *If you want different results, don't do the same things.*

– *You won't solve your problems with the same mindset you had when you created them.*

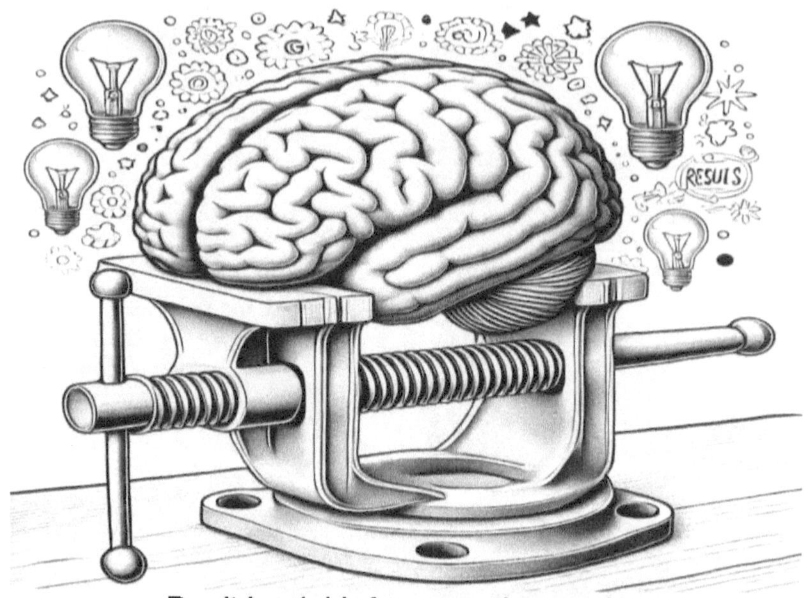

Don't be rigid, focus on the results.

Generally, there are multiple valid ways to achieve the same goal, so it is not necessary to restrict oneself to a single option. As long as you respect your own and others' rights, you can choose any method that offers good results. Additionally, if the adopted procedures start to generate unsatisfactory consequences, it is advisable to consider changing them.

−*Don't fear necessary changes.*

FINAL CONSIDERATIONS

Strength is the firmness or ability to maintain the resolutions made, despite internal and external pressures, in the circumstances and manner necessary to do so.

At one of its vicious extremes lies the weakness of will, characterized by a lack of energy in resolutions, making it difficult or impossible to maintain them. Even knowing how to act, such individuals end up behaving differently.

At the other vicious extreme is the rigidity of those who have difficulties learning from experience and modifying their decisions when necessary, leading to the repetition of the same mistakes over and over again.

~~~

Chapter 5. COURAGE

Courage is a component of strength that consists of the ability to overcome fear, in the circumstances and in the way it is necessary to do so.

−I am afraid, but I will do it because I must.

On the other hand, fear is an emotional state experienced as unease, alarm, or insecurity. It appears when an individual feels threatened because they perceive the possibility of suffering some harm. This perception does not depend on whether the situation to be faced is actually dangerous, but on whether it is considered so, rightly or wrongly.[180]

Is it necessary to avoid it at all costs? Fear, in its proper place, time, and measure, is the mother of caution. It prepares us to face situations that are considered threatening or dangerous and is productive to the extent that it allows us to mobilize our resources and prepare for a physical and mental performance appropriate to the magnitude of the demand.[181] Its effect becomes unproductive when it causes paralysis in circumstances where action is needed, makes us avoid situations that should be faced, or leads to completely disorganized and uncontrolled behavior.

It is important to highlight that avoiding a problem or threat does not necessarily imply a lack of courage; sometimes, getting to safety is the most prudent action. The brave person overcomes their fear in the circumstances and in the manner necessary, facing what must be faced, and avoiding what should be avoided.

−Avoiding unnecessary danger is not cowardice, but prudence.

The absence of fear is not synonymous with courage, as one might lack it due to ignorance or an inability to feel it because of some drug or mental illness. Under such conditions, the individual will lack its benefits.

It is also necessary to differentiate between being fearful and being cowardly. A fearful person is afraid of many things that most of their peers do not fear, and having to face a greater number of fears makes it more difficult for them to be brave.

Courage, Success, and Maintaining What Has Been Achieved

The path to success is filled with situations that can be considered threatening, and once it is achieved, dangers will not be lacking. Therefore, courage is essential to achieve and maintain it.

−Fortune favors the bold. (Spain) [182]

−Fortune helps the audacious. (Fortune audaces iuvat, Virgil) [183]

Daring

A quality closely related to courage is daring, which consists of deciding to undertake a risky action where there is a possibility of harm or failure.

Who does not dare to cross a stream. How will they cross a lake? (Tibet) [184]

In life, uncertainty prevails over certainty. When we embark on a new venture, we always run the risk of not succeeding, but often the only way to know the outcome of our actions is by taking a risk.

−*Every attempt carries the risk of failure.*

−*Every gain has its risks.*

−*To win, you have to risk.*

−*Who does not venture does not cross the sea. (Spain)* [185]

−*He who does not risk an egg, does not get a chicken. (Panama)* [186]

−*He who did not venture, neither lost nor won.*

When it comes to taking risks, it is just as harmful to be overcome by inertia and fear as it is to undertake actions hastily without due reflection. Sometimes, the most appropriate decision after careful deliberation may be not to take the risk. In fact, there are risks that simply should not be taken.

−*There are risks that are better avoided.*

COWARDICE

He who lacks courage needs legs. (Italy) [187]

One of the vicious extremes of courage is cowardice, which consists of the inability to overcome fear in the circumstances and in the manner necessary.

−Cowardice is fear indulged, while courage is fear mastered.

The coward opts for the easy and seductive path of avoiding harm, at the expense of their principles, which is why this moral vice is often accompanied by feelings of guilt or remorse.

−The coward eventually does what they do not want, dominated by fear.

Cowardice incapacitates a person from achieving lofty goals.

−No one reached the summit accompanied by cowardice.

−A cowardly man does not enter the palace.

−Nothing has been written about cowards.

This quality impoverishes the existence of those who possess it.

−He who falters in danger does not even earn his meal. (Argentina)[188]

−The coward dies many times before dying.

−...woe to cowardly hearts and idle hands! (Ecclesiasticus 2:12)[189]

−Acting from fear, our life will become increasingly poorer.

TEMERITY

He who seeks danger perishes in it. (Panama)[190]

The other vicious extreme of courage is the recklessness of those who expose themselves to unnecessary dangers, often suffering the undesirable effects of their actions.

- *He who exposes himself to a useless danger dies a martyr of the devil. (Netherlands)[191]*
- *The fish that seeks the hook seeks its doom. (Spain)[192]*
- *The wife of a careless man almost always ends up a widow. (Hungary)[193]*
- *He who does not take care of himself does not know his grandchildren. (Afro-Cuban saying)[194]*
- *Danger comes more quickly when it is despised.*

Look before you leap. (England)[195]

Courage is not contrary to caution, which consists of preventing inconveniences, harm, or dangers in order to avoid or face them in the best possible way.

—*Better to be safe than sorry. (Czechoslovakia)[196]*

—*Do not sign a letter you haven't read, nor drink water you haven't seen. (Spain)[197]*

—*Better a "just in case" than a "who would have known?" (Cuba)[198]*

—*It's better to be cautious than to have regrets. (Spain)[199]*

FINAL CONSIDERATIONS

Courage is the ability to overcome fear in the circumstances and in the way it is necessary to do so.

Fear makes it possible for an individual to prepare to face what they consider threatening or dangerous. Its effect is unproductive if it paralyzes when action is needed, makes one avoid situations that must be faced, or disorganizes behavior. Neither the absence of fear is synonymous with courage, nor its presence with cowardice.

A quality closely related to courage is daring, which consists of deciding to undertake a risky action where there is a possibility of harm or failure.

One of the vicious extremes of courage is the cowardice of those who are unable to overcome their fears in the circumstances and in the manner necessary.

At the other vicious extreme is the recklessness of those who expose themselves to unnecessary dangers, or necessary ones but without due consideration or examination of these.

~~~

Chapter 6: PATIENCE

He who is patient will endure as long as necessary, and in the end, his reward will be joy. (Ecclesiasticus 1:23)[200]

Patience is the ability to overcome oneself in the face of the sufferings and discomforts of a necessary wait, and in this sense, it constitutes knowing how to wait wisely.

- *Patience is bitter, but its fruits are sweet. (France)[201]*

- *Being patient is a sign of great intelligence; being impatient is a sign of great stupidity. (Proverbs 14:29)[202]*

Suffering is an inevitable component of life, and knowing how to face it is one of the elements that define the moral culture of a human being.

- *...the value of gold is tested in fire, and the value of men in the furnace of suffering. (Ecclesiasticus 2:5)[203]*

Suffering is also an opportunity to know oneself and to mature. We grow from it, overcoming losses, resolving conflicts, and solving problems.

- *He who does not fall does not get up. (Spain)[204]*

- *No one has grown without having suffered.*

- *He who has not been tested knows little. (Ecclesiasticus 34:10)[205]*

Despite the positive and even necessary effect of suffering in our lives, it can drive us to actions completely inappropriate to our purposes by making a wait truly difficult to endure.

Where can the causes of sufferings and discomforts during a necessary wait be found? In circumstances that can be truly rigorous for most people, or the individual may have some particular weakness in enduring them. Also, a great motivation and burning desire to obtain what is awaited can make its absence difficult to endure.

There are several elements that increase our ability to endure the sufferings and discomforts of a necessary wait, and thus increase the chances of having patience, including the presence of sufficient desire to achieve the proposed goals.

—Desire makes the ugly beautiful. (Spain)[206]

—He who has no desire, everything hurts. (Czechoslovakia)[207]

—He who wants to do something finds a way; he who does not, finds excuses.

But desires should not be so excessive that the absence of what is desired becomes unbearable.

—Neither with all the hunger to the chest, nor with all the thirst to the pitcher. (Spain)[208]

—Control your desires or they will control you.

There must be clarity about the goals for which one suffers and the conviction that they can be achieved, which would give meaning to the suffering; it would no longer be for nothing, or for something that has a high probability of not being obtained, thus it would not be an unnecessary or wasted suffering.

It is necessary to have a clear or approximate idea of the time that will be required to wait and the hardships that will have to be endured.

—The patience of the farmer is born of his hope.

—Patience sustains hope, and hope maintains patience.

The opposite happens when there are doubts about the attainability of the goal, or great uncertainty about when the uncomfortable situation will end.

Finally, when waiting for something eagerly, one should avoid fighting against time. Instead of suffering by wishing it would pass faster, it is advisable to fill that space with other goals and activities that enrich our lives and distract us from the discomfort of waiting.

—Let's make use of time instead of fighting against it.

—There is a way to beat time, and that is by making the most of it.

The fruit grows slowly. (India)[209]

Every good result needs time to come to fruition.

- *The orange ripens in its own time. (Cuba)[210]*
- *The hard pear matures with time.*
- *Every good thing requires time to achieve.*
- *Every process takes its own time.*

Because of this, knowing how to wait is an ingredient of extraordinary importance for achieving success and ensuring excellent quality in the products we create.

Patience and success

He who knew how to wait, arrives at triumph.

Although this quality is not the only one necessary to achieve successful results, it is essential.

−*Patience is the key to paradise. (Turkey)*[211]

−*The world belongs to the patient man. (Italy)*[212]

−*Fortune surrenders to those who know how to wait wisely.*

−*A moment of patience, ten years of comfort. (Greece)*[213]

−*With patience and a little stick, even the green ones fall. (Cuba)*[214]

−*The snake doesn't catch the hen by running, but by watching.*

−*Skill and patience triumph where force fails.*

Patience and quality of the products that are made

Slow work produces the finest articles. (China)[215]

Excellence in any activity is usually achieved only after dedicating a great amount of time and effort, especially if this continuous practice is focused on constant improvement and surpassing one's own limits.[216]

–Patience and the mulberry leaf make the silk robe. (China)[217]

–Pearls that are not polished do not shine. (Japan)[218]

Events are like fruits; you must eat them neither a day
before they are ripe nor a day after. (José Martí) [219]

To achieve desired goals, it is very important to wait for the right circumstances to act in a certain way, which is nothing other than timing.

–*Acting at the right time is triumph. (Arab proverb)*[220]

–*In this world, everything has its hour; there is a time for everything that happens. (Ecclesiastes 3:1)*[221]

–*Everything in its own time. (Czech proverb)*[222]

One must wait for chance to create opportunities when we cannot or should not create them ourselves; otherwise, it would be more beneficial to help these opportunities form. In fact, waiting is a form of action, and doing so wisely means continuing to do what is necessary.

– *Patience without diligence is a ruinous virtue and vain knowledge.*

– *To win: patience and skill.*

There is success when opportunity and the ability to seize it coincide, so it is not only necessary to wait for favorable circumstances or help them form but also to prepare ourselves to take advantage of them. In this sense, we must be diligent.

– *Skill counts for very little without opportunity, and opportunity counts for very little without the skill to seize it.*[223]

– *Chance only favors the prepared mind.*

IMPATIENCE

The cat always catches the impatient mouse.
(Morocco)[224]

One of the vicious extremes of patience is impatience, which consists of the inability to overcome oneself in the face of the rigors of a necessary wait. Acting from impatience often leads to disorganized or premature actions, frustrating many intentions.

– *A little impatience ruins great plans. (China)225*

– *He who has no patience has nothing. (Italy)226*

– *Where there is no patience, there is no skill.*

A very common consequence of impatience is haste, which involves rushing into action or speech without any consideration. This can arise from an inability to endure the discomforts of waiting or from a burning desire to obtain what one has been waiting for. It can also come from a lack of knowledge about when the right time to act is, or from the habit of acting thoughtlessly.

Whatever the cause, the result could be: failures, lack of quality in decisions or in the products created, delays in achieving goals, or abandonment of efforts.

Precipitation and failure

Acting without thinking is like shooting without aiming.

Because the hasty person acts before being prepared or before the circumstances are favorable, they spoil their intentions.

- *Haste is the father of failure.*

- *He who rushes delays or loses.*

- *Acting without thinking can make us stumble.*

- *Enthusiasm without knowledge is not good; haste makes mistakes. (Proverbs 19:2)*[227]

Haste and Poor Quality of Our Decisions

Since hasty decisions are thoughtless, they often bring some type of undesirable consequence that we may regret.

- *He who makes sudden decisions, suddenly regrets. (Spain)*[228]

- *He who promises quickly, fulfills slowly and regrets quickly. (Spain)*[229]

Precipitation and poor quality of the products we produce

A hurried building is ruinous.

A project planned in haste, executed with rushed actions, or completed without dedicating the time and effort required for a good finish will inevitably have deficiencies.

– *Quickly and well almost never go together.*

– *Hasty work is rarely worth much. (Czechoslovakia)*[230]

– *He who cooks in haste eats raw.*

– *Hasty work falls from the hands. (Czechoslovakia)*[231]

Haste and Delay

A very common consequence of haste is delay.

– *Haste is slow. (Latin proverb)*[232]

– *He who hurries too much ends up late.*

– *If you don't do things well due to haste, you'll have to do them again.*

The cart does not go before the oxen. (Afro-Cuban saying)[233]

Why does this happen? To achieve any goal, it is necessary to go through stages in a specific order, as each one prepares us for the next.

- *How are you going to paint the house if the foundations haven't been laid yet?*
- *Don't start building the house from the roof. (Mexico)[234]*
- *Don't try to cross the bridge before you reach the river.*
- *Don't try to reach the summit before climbing the mountain.*
- *Don't attempt to start at the end.*
- *Many of our failures come from trying to hasten the time of success.*

The hasty person acts recklessly, as in their urgency, they do not pay proper attention to what they are doing; and the very speed they impose on their actions could exceed their ability to react, making them prone to mistakes.

- *In hasty action, one loses control of oneself. (Lao Tzu)[235]*
- *Excessive speed exposes us to error.*
- *For the one in a hurry, a small obstacle becomes a big one.*

By attempting to take actions without having first done those that should have been executed beforehand, the hasty person disrupts the order in which the stages should have been completed to reach their goals. As a result, they must waste time and effort to backtrack and redirect their efforts in the correct order, if they haven't already ruined everything.

– *Anything that forces evolution is destroying it.*

– *Do things well so you don't have to redo them. (Afro-Cuban saying)[236]*

No matter how urgent the situation, it is advisable to keep a cool head and pay the necessary attention to what is being done.

– *Make haste slowly. (Latin proverb)[237]*

– *Dress slowly when you are in a hurry. (France)[238]*

There is a time to walk slowly and a time to walk quickly.

It is necessary to clarify that it is not about always walking slowly, as there are circumstances that require quick actions. One should walk quickly or slowly according to the demands of the circumstances.

–*Going quickly has its advantages, going slowly has its advantages. (African saying)[239]*

Precipitation and abandonment

He who has traveled the desert knows that the man who walks without haste will arrive before the one who runs. (Persian poet Saadi)[240]

Due to impatience and haste, one may undertake endeavors without considering their demands, possible discomforts, and whether or not one is prepared to face and endure them. Thus, when the rigor of these is perceived, the individual may feel tempted to abandon the effort or be truly forced to do so.

– *He who runs too much, stops soon. (Spain)[241]*

PASSIVITY AND OBSTINACY

At the other vicious extreme of patience is the passivity of those who unnecessarily endure unfavorable circumstances and irritating characteristics of others, which they have the right not to tolerate.

– *We don't have to endure everything.*

– *Life is to be lived, not just endured.*

Sometimes you have to change direction; waiting is
not always the solution.

At this extreme, there is also the stubbornness or obstinacy of those who continue waiting for something, despite the senseless and unproductive nature of the wait.

– *One thing is to be patient, another is to waste time.*

– *I'm not in a hurry, but I also don't want to waste time.*

– *Don't get mad at the dry well that doesn't give you water; instead, ask yourself: why do I keep insisting on drawing water from where it's clear there is none?*

– *Don't look where there is nothing.*

– *In life, some doors close so that you change direction.*

FINAL CONSIDERATIONS

Patience is the ability to overcome oneself in the face of the sufferings and discomforts of a necessary wait. Among the elements that increase the chances of having it are:

- *Sufficient desire to achieve the proposed goals.*
- *Clarity about the goals for which one suffers and conviction that they can be obtained.*
- *Precision or an approximate idea of the time needed to wait and the hardships to be endured to achieve the proposed goals.*
- *The right attitude that allows making the most of time instead of fighting against it.*

One of the vicious extremes of this quality is the impatience of those who are unable to overcome themselves in the face of the rigors of a necessary wait, which causes haste, and this, in turn, leads to failures, poor quality in the products created, delays, and abandonment.

At the other vicious extreme are the passivity of those who endure unfavorable circumstances and irritating characteristics of others, which they have the right not to tolerate; and the stubbornness and obstinacy of those who continue waiting for something despite the senseless and unproductive nature of the wait.

~~~

Chapter 7. PERSEVERANCE

He who perseveres triumphs, and he who is determined achieves. (Afro-Cuban saying)[242]

Perseverance is the firmness in your purposes, despite internal and external obstacles. It is not the only quality necessary for success, but without it, being successful is impossible.

– *In constancy lies the most secure support of human ambitions.*

– *Good things come to those who have perseverance.*

– *Perseverance is crowned with success.*

–*A component of perseverance is the ability to make the necessary changes in means and objectives.*

Ability to Change

What is the importance of knowing how to change, and what are its limits? Our methods for achieving our goals will be effective and efficient as long as the circumstances are favorable. When these circumstances change unfavorably and we do not adapt, we will fail.

– *Success comes to those whose methods adapt to changing circumstances, and failure comes to those who do the opposite.*

– I decide according to the circumstances of the time, and I act accordingly. (Confucius)[243]

– Put on your cloak according to the wind. (Spain)[244]

When the land does not yield, prepare to move.

On the other hand, due to changing circumstances, certain goals that were perfectly attainable may cease to be so, requiring adjustments that might even include abandoning those goals.

– A clever farmer does not till land that does not bear fruit. (Spain)[245]

– A business that does not profit should be abandoned.

– Don't look where there is nothing. (Spain)[246]

– If something does not move forward, let it go and move forward yourself.

Effectiveness and efficiency are important but not sufficient. Another criterion for changing or maintaining methods and goals is respecting the rights of others and oneself, which constitutes the limit of the previous two criteria.

Without the ability to change methods, means, and goals, perseverance degenerates into obstinacy.

Perseverance as an essential quality to achieve goals that require a lot of time and effort

Drop by drop, the leak wears through. (Spain)[247]

Perseverance is of vital importance for achieving goals that require a long time and considerable effort to reach. Many goals are not achieved in one single stroke but little by little. On the path to these goals, an individual will encounter numerous internal and external obstacles that they must overcome or circumvent.

– *Zamora was not won in an hour. (Spain)[248]*

– *One single blow does not bring down an oak. (Spain)[249]*

– *Drop by drop, the sea drains away. (Galicia, Spain)[250]*

– *Put a grain each day, and soon you will have a heap. (Spain)[251]*

– *Grain by grain, the granary fills up. (Spain)[252]*

– *One grain does not make a granary, but it helps its neighbor. (Spain)[253]*

INCONSTANCY

He whose spirit is as inconsistent as milk foam builds nothing lasting in life. (Tuareg Arab saying) [254]

Inconstancy is the lack of firmness in purposes when facing obstacles, which can be internal, external, or both.

– *The fool has no fixed goal. (Proverbs 17:24)*[255]

Without firmness in purposes, one will not dedicate the necessary time and energy to their achievement, and thus they will not be attained.

– *Without application, there is no reward.*

– *Without perseverance, talent is barren soil. (England)*[256]

OBSTINACY

Obstinacy is a form of rigidity, which consists of the inability to reconsider goals or means, or to abandon them, despite their senselessness, thus persisting in error.

Obstinacy appears, firstly, when a primary goal needs to be modified, relegated to lower priority by other objectives, or abandoned, but the individual is unable to do so.

Secondly, it appears when overcoming a difficult or impossible obstacle on the path to achieving a goal becomes so important to the individual that it turns into a primary goal, and the initial objective and the reasons behind the actions are relegated to lower priority.[257]

Causes of Persistence in Error

There are several reasons why an individual may persist in the error of incorrect goals or means, including:

Erroneous Learning: The individual may become accustomed to procedures that do not lead to the proposed goals. Even with other options available, it is more comfortable to persist in what they are accustomed to than to change their behavior.

−*Custom is a second nature.*[258]

−*Custom sometimes makes us live in a cage, even knowing that the door is open.*

Incorrect Education: The individual may become used to always having their will fulfilled, resulting in making persistence in error a willful act, with the fundamental motive being: "I want it to be this way."

−*A mother who indulges raises a serpent. (Mexico)*[259]

−*An overly pious mother is a harmful mother. (Spain)*[260]

Lack of Knowledge of Other Ways to Achieve the Proposed Goals, or the Fact That One Can and Should Consider Other Goals.

−*Ignorance knocks one down in the struggle. (Guinea)*[261]

−*The ignorant and the blind walk gropingly.*

−*He who does not know is like he who does not see. (Spain)*[262]

Due to intense emotional states that prevent clear thinking and awareness of the error.

− *Passion blinds reason.*

− *When passions blind, reasoning is unnecessary.*

− *Where the heart is king, its order cannot be disobeyed. (Afro-Cuban saying)*[263]

Due to a specific fear of change and the new, where the individual prefers to continue in a precarious situation that they know well and that provides a certain sense of security, rather than deciding to change and face the risks that any change entails.

−*The bird that falls to the ground while trying its first flight is not mistaken, but the one that renounces flying out of fear of falling.*

−*If you do not dare to lose sight of the shore, you will not be able to conquer new horizons.*

Because a lot of time, effort, or other resources have been invested in achieving incorrect goals, and one continues to persist in the error almost as a tribute to the time, effort, or resources used.

—No matter how long you have been walking in the wrong direction, you can always turn around.

Because of not wanting to admit to others that one is wrong, even when fully aware of the error.

—Pride never says, "I was wrong."

—He who only seeks to prove he is right, ends up being wrong.

Secondary gain. For the individual, some outcome of their persistence in error may be very attractive, such as abandoning responsibilities or obtaining affection from family and friends, which they would have to give up if they corrected their course.

—He who chooses to be an ox, licks the yoke. (Mexico)[264]

—When you like the itch, it doesn't bother you, and if it does, it doesn't distress you. (Cuba)[265]

—It doesn't count as hell if you like the way it burns.

Psychological rigidity due to some biological damage to the brain or its coverings.

Mixed causes, involving more than one of the previously explained factors.

Regardless of the cause of persistence in error, it will always bring bad consequences.

Consequences of persisting in error

You must be willing to abandon false paths.

The fundamental consequence of persisting in error is repeating the same negative experiences and obtaining the same results until the lesson is learned.

– Until you change, you will keep repeating the same experiences.

If, in trying to achieve a goal using certain methods and under certain circumstances, you obtain negative results, but you continue trying to achieve the same goal with the same methods and circumstances, it follows that you will keep obtaining the same negative results.

– If you don't change, everything repeats.

– Don't expect different results if you keep doing the same thing.

– For different results: different actions.

– Don't get mad at the dry well because it doesn't give you water; instead, ask yourself why you keep insisting on drawing water from where it's clear you can't find any.

FINAL CONSIDERATIONS

Perseverance is the firmness in one's purposes despite internal and external obstacles.

At one of its vicious extremes lies the inconstancy of those who lack firmness in their purposes and give up when obstacles arise in the pursuit of their resolutions.

At the other extreme is the obstinacy of those who are incapable of reconsidering or abandoning their goals or methods, despite their senselessness.

Among the causes of persistence in error are:

Erroneous Learning: The individual may become accustomed to procedures that do not lead to the proposed goals. Even with other options available, it is more comfortable to persist in what they are used to than to change their behavior.

Incorrect Education: The individual may become used to always having their will fulfilled, resulting in making persistence in error a willful act, with the fundamental motive being: "I want it to be this way."

Lack of Knowledge: Not knowing other ways to achieve the proposed goals, or that one can and should consider other goals.

Intense Emotional States: These prevent clear thinking and awareness of the error.

Fear of Change: A specific fear of change and the new, where the individual prefers to continue in a precarious situation that they know well and that provides a certain sense of security, rather than deciding to change and face the risks that any change entails.

Investment of Resources: Because a lot of time, effort, or other resources have been invested in achieving incorrect goals, and one continues to persist in the error almost as a tribute to the time, effort, or resources used.

Reluctance to Admit Error: Not wanting to admit to others that one is wrong, even when fully aware of the error.

Secondary Gain: For the individual, some outcome of their persistence in error may be very attractive, such as abandoning responsibilities or obtaining affection and attention from family and friends, which they would have to give up or receive less of if they corrected their course.

Psychological Rigidity: Due to some biological damage to the brain or its coverings.

Mixed Causes: Involving more than one of the previously explained factors.

The fundamental consequence of persisting in error is repeating the same negative experiences and obtaining the same results until the lesson is learned.

~~~

Chapter 8. EQUANIMITY

Equanimity consists of the steadiness and constancy of mind and serene impartiality of judgment, despite changes in favorable or unfavorable fortune.

– *In moments of satisfaction or fury, you see a man's level of moral culture. (China)*[266]

Elements of equanimity include the ability to avoid despair and dejection, knowing how to face both adversity and prosperity, not becoming complacent when success seems imminent, understanding the impermanence of things, and the ability to seek the best mental state for making decisions.

Avoid despair and despondency

Banging your head will not hollow out the wall. (Czech Republic)[267]

Two very unproductive responses to adversity are despair and dejection, both of which only serve to increase bad fortune. The first generally results in hasty actions that can worsen the situation.

– *He who despairs in misfortune increases it. (Panchatantra)*[268]

– *If you lose your head in difficult situations, you will only make things worse.*

– He who loses his head, loses himself. (Afro-Cuban saying)[269]

– Despair remedies nothing.

– Shouting will not extinguish the fire. (Czechoslovakia)[270]

– The more you grieve, the greater your loss. (Persian saying)[271]

Dejection, on the other hand, causes one to lose energy and abandon efforts to overcome setbacks.

– A good tree does not fall at the first blow. (Germany)[272]

– If you become discouraged when in trouble, your strength is not much. (Proverbs 24:10)[273]

– Do not let yourself be overcome by the inevitable storms of life.

Knowing how to face both adversity and prosperity

When prosperity is riding high, loosen the reins and soon you will fall from the saddle. (Benjamin Franklin)[274]

The moral culture of a human being is revealed in both facing adversity and handling prosperity. It's clear that moral virtues are needed to face adversity, but in times of prosperity, humans tend to relax and neglect the necessary discipline and precautions, often resulting in misfortune.

−*He who is not a true man cannot endure either poverty or prosperity for long. (Confucius)*[275]

−*In prosperity, prudence; in adversity, patience. (Netherlands)*[276]

−*Neither exalt yourself in wealth nor abase yourself in poverty.*

−*In prosperity be cautious; in adversity be patient. (Portugal)*[277]

−*In times of good fortune or adversity, you see... if a man has a great mind or a small one. (China)*[278]

Not to relax in the face of the proximity of a success that seems imminent

From the plate to the mouth, the soup can spill.

When success seems imminent, it is necessary to maintain proper care until the triumph is fully achieved. Confusing the nearness of victory with the actual victory can cause relaxation and often defeat.

−*Human affairs are often damaged when they are about to be completed. By being careful both at the beginning and the end, failure is avoided. (Lao Tzu)*[279]

−*Don't count your chickens before they hatch.*

−*Don't praise yourself before you finish. (Spain)*[280]

−*Don't sing glory until the victory is won. (Spain)*[281]

Understanding the Impermanence of Things

Generally, when someone is going through a difficult or fortunate situation, they tend to think that all their days will be like this. However, circumstances and individuals constantly evolve and change.

- *A happy day makes one forget misfortunes, and a bad day makes one forget happiness. (Ecclesiasticus 11:25)[282]*
- *Everything passes, nothing is permanent.*
- *Bad times don't last forever; neither do good times.*

Life has its ups and downs.

A human's life is not like their worst or best day but oscillates constantly. There will be days with reasons for sadness and others for joy, and both success and failure, happiness and sorrow are temporary.

- *Joy and anger, happiness and sorrow, worries and troubles, indecisions and fears, hover over us in turn, in everchanging forms. (Chuang Tzu)[283]*
- *...The wise man... examines fullness and decline; therefore, he neither rejoices in success nor laments in failure, because he knows that conditions are not constant. (Chuang Tzu)[284]*
- *All good and bad things come to an end. (Spain)[285]*
- *Life is much more than a moment of despair or joy.*

Whenever it rains, it clears up, and whenever it clears
up, it will rain again.

The world does not stop when we achieve a goal, nor when we fail.

- *It never rained without stopping, nor stopped without raining.*

- *After the storm comes the calm. (Spain)*[286]

- *No matter how long the storm lasts, the sun always shines again between the clouds.*

- *Nothing is eternal, neither what you love nor what hurts you.*

- *Every night has its dawn, and every day its dusk. Everything passes.*

Seeking a Better Mental State to Decide

Before making important decisions, calm yourself first.

When dominated by emotion or passion, clear thinking is compromised, and decisions made in such a state are generally incorrect. This is why an important element of equanimity is the ability to seek or wait for the best possible mental state for deliberating and making decisions.

– *Do not make decisions in moments of desolation.*

– *Do not answer a letter when you are hungry.*

When we are disturbed by anger, the heart is not in its proper place; when blinded by love, the heart is not in its proper place; when enveloped by worries and anxieties, the heart is not in its proper place, the spirit has lost its balance. (Confucius)[287]

– *When the emotional sea is very agitated, do not make major decisions. Keep silent and wait for the storm to pass.*

For Confucius, this optimal state for deliberation is called "central harmony":

– *When passions such as joy, anger, and pleasure have not awakened, that is our central or moral self. When these passions awaken and each achieves its proper degree and measure, that is harmony... (Confucius)[288]*

– *Achieving central harmony is certainly the most significant human conquest. For a long time, people have been very unable to achieve it. (Confucius)[289]*

IMPULSIVENESS AND INCONTINENCE

At one of the vicious extremes of equanimity are impulsiveness, which was conceptually defined in the section on imprudence, and incontinence, which was conceptualized in the section on weakness of will.

He who is impulsive acts without thinking; he who is reflective remains calm. (Proverbs 14:17)[290]

Both impulsiveness and incontinence result in inappropriate actions, but the impulsive person acts without thinking about the consequences of their actions or words, making this vice more akin to imprudence. The incontinent person, on the other hand, knows the consequences of their actions and knows that such behavior is wrong, but still cannot restrain themselves and say "No" to themselves, which is a form of weakness of will. It is not uncommon for a person to suffer from both vices simultaneously.

> *– Like a city without walls and exposed to danger, so is he who cannot control his impulses. (Proverbs 25:28)[291]*

IMPASSIVENESS

At the other extreme of equanimity lies the impassiveness of those who are indifferent to situations that warrant their interest and attention.

FINAL CONSIDERATIONS

Equanimity is the steadiness of mind and serene impartiality of judgment, despite changes in favorable or unfavorable fortune.

At one of the vicious extremes of equanimity are impulsiveness, as conceptualized in the section on imprudence, and incontinence, as defined in the section on weakness of will.

At the other extreme of equanimity is the impassiveness of those who are indifferent to situations that warrant their interest and attention.

~~~

Chapter 9. RESIGNATION

This quality consists of acceptance and compliance with situations or conditions that the individual cannot, or can, but should not, change to improve.

– Accept that which cannot be changed.

It's no use crying over spilled milk. (England)[292]

Why is resignation important? There are situations that are irreparable and losses that are irreplaceable, where the only solution is to accept them and rebuild one's life based on the new situation.

– Knowing how to suffer makes suffering less.

– When something cannot be corrected, the best thing is to know how to endure it. (Seneca)[293]

– What cannot be remedied, it's best to forget. (Spain)[294]

– Where there is no remedy, there should be resignation.

Sometimes, an individual has so much trouble overcoming an irreplaceable loss that they make it the center of their existence. In addition to unnecessarily prolonging their suffering, they will have difficulties moving forward and rebuilding their life based on their new reality.[295]

– Tears do not let you see the road. (India)[296]

– If you look back too much, you will reach nowhere. (Mexico)[297]

– He who does not look ahead stays behind. (Spain)[298]

– Look forward so that you do not stay behind. (Benjamin Franklin)[299]

– Not to progress is to regress. (Latin Proverb: Non progredi est regredi)[300]

It's not about being immune to pain and feeling perfectly fine immediately after suffering a significant loss, especially if it is unexpected. Just as a physical wound does not heal instantly but takes a few days to mend and scar, acceptance does not come all at once but is a process of assimilation that also requires time.

– Respect the processes.

– Do not rush what needs time to grow.

The greatness of a human being does not lie in not suffering from life's severe blows but in knowing how to get up and continue living despite them. It is what you do with the pain that makes the difference.

– By the power to rise, men are measured. (José Martí)[301]

– If you fall seven times, get up eight.

– Falling is optional, getting up is mandatory.

There is always a lesson to be learned from losses. At the very least, they put us in a better position to console someone going through a similar situation. And if we are wise, they will teach us to avoid those that are avoidable and to prepare ourselves as best as possible to face and overcome those that are not.

– He who chooses to move forward instead of suffering indefinitely will always emerge stronger.

– Every battle serves to teach us something, even the ones we lose.

– Look your problem in the face and ask it: What do you want to teach me?

– When it hurts, just observe: life is trying to teach you something.

It's important to clarify that resignation does not mean accepting everything. This would be passivity and conformism, which prevent us from changing and growing as individuals. Resignation involves not accepting and diligently modifying what should be changed, as long as it is done in the circumstances and in the manner in which it is necessary.

– Change the things that must be changed. (Latin Proverb: Mutatis mutandis)[302]

The wise man thinks about his troubles when it leads
to something practical.

But not accepting what needs to be changed is useless if it doesn't translate into actions and only exists in our minds as anxieties and worries.

- *Time should not be wasted in suffering; it should be used to fulfill our duty. (José Martí)[303]*

- *Let's think about our problems to find solutions, not to torment ourselves.*

- *When facing problems, don't worry, take action. (Mexico)[304]*

It is important that we work diligently to solve our problems, doing what depends on us and remaining calm about the rest.

- *Do what is right and let things fall into place.*

- *Do your diligence, and let God act as He will.*

- *If it's not in your hands, let it not be in your mind.*

A version of the previous idea, which reverses its order, emphasizes that despite having resources that give us calm, we should be active and diligent in relation to what depends on us:

- *Trust in the Virgin, but run. (Spain)[305]*

- *Pray to God, but keep rowing towards the shore. (Russia)[306]*

- *Trust in God, but tie your camels.*

- *Praying to God while striking with the hammer. (Spain)[307]*

CONFORMISM

Conformity is the enemy of growth.

One of the vicious extremes of resignation is conformity, which consists of accepting and being content with situations or conditions that harm us and that we can improve.

- *If you crawl like a worm, don't complain if you get stepped on.*
- *When you settle, you give up the opportunity to be better.*

DISCONTENT

Nothing satisfies the discontented. (Cuba)[308]

At the other vicious extreme of resignation is the discontentment of those who are hostile to everything established in the political, social, moral, aesthetic order, etc.

- *It is a bad disease not to be content with anything.*

- *The discontented person, if given gold earrings, says they are heavy. (Cuba)[309]*

A nuance of discontentment is that it makes a person live focused on what they lack, so they enjoy little or nothing of what they do have.

- *The mirage of what we lack blinds us to what we have in abundance.*

- *Sometimes we are so busy chasing what we lack that we forget to enjoy what we already have.*

- *If you focus on what you lack, you won't be able to enjoy what you do have.*

It's about focusing on what we have and can do, and finding a balance between wanting more and taking the time to enjoy what we already have.

- *Focus on what you do have, on what there is, on what you can do.*

- *Be happy with what you have while pursuing what you want.*

If you cry at night because the sun is absent, you won't
see the stars.

A manifestation of discontent is the habit of frequent complaining, often without significant reason. The complainer, instead of enjoying all the good and pleasurable things in their life, focuses on its negative aspects.

- *Complaints about what you don't have prevent you from enjoying what you already possess.*

- *Don't waste the good by complaining about the bad.*

But constant complaining neither solves problems nor makes life more beautiful.

- *Complaining about life doesn't improve it.*

- *Complaints bore others and don't solve problems.*

Complaining actually worsens problems for several reasons, among them that when an individual is focused on the negative and on their complaints, they don't engage in seeking solutions.

- *With half the energy a complainer uses to craft a complaint, one could start building a solution.*

- *It's better to light a candle than to curse the darkness.*

- *When something bothers you, if you can change it, do so; if you can't, accept it, but don't keep complaining.*

- *Either change it or accept it. Stop complaining.*

– Stop complaining and start resolving.

Generally, the life led by a complainer is the envy of many others who have much less.

– When you are about to complain, think of the people who are happy with less than you have.

– Your life is the dream of many who have much less than you.

Thus, you might feel more satisfied if you were a bit more grateful for what you have.

– Smile more and complain less. There is much to be thankful for.

– Life says to stop complaining and enjoy it, because it will pass anyway.

FINAL CONSIDERATIONS

Resignation is the acceptance of what cannot or should not be changed, while changing what should be changed.

One of its vicious extremes is the conformity of those who accept situations or conditions that they can and should change to improve.

At the other extreme is the discontent of those who are hostile to everything established in the political, social, moral, aesthetic order, etc., and as a manifestation of this, the frequent complaining of those who often complain without significant reason.

~~~

Chapter 10. INTERACTION BETWEEN THE CARDINAL VIRTUES

This interaction will be approached from the conception of the golden mean, according to which ethical-moral qualities occupy an intermediate position between vicious extremes, one of excess and the other of deficiency. This is quite evident for fortitude and its components. Although justice, moderation, and prudence only have one extreme—injustice, intemperance, and imprudence respectively—there are particular forms of these unique deviations caused by the existence of another special vice that does have both extremes. For example, one can be unjust due to either leniency or cruelty.

Each of the cardinal virtues is necessary for the proper functioning of the others, and disturbances in any of them will inevitably produce corruptions in the others.

Prudence and Justice

If the objectives are ethically incorrect in the sense that they cause unjustified harm to others or to the individual pursuing them, one will be unjust.

 Pursue the best ends with the best means.

If one has good objectives but intends to achieve them through ethically incorrect means, prudence degenerates into cunning and wickedness, which ultimately isolates the individual.

- *You can fool some people some of the time, but not all the people all the time. (Afro-Cuban saying)*[310]

- *You can be more cunning than one person, but not more cunning than everyone else. (Afro-Cuban saying)*[311]

Justice without prudence degenerates into injustice, as to be just, it is necessary to determine one's own and others' rights and the best ways to assert them.

- *If you do not know the rights that belong to you, you cannot claim them. (Afro-Cuban saying)*[312]

Fortitude and Justice

The fortitude needed to achieve the goals set by an individual will be ethically and morally correct if it is exercised while respecting the rights of others and oneself, thus necessitating justice. In fact, fortitude without justice degenerates into cruelty, which becomes evident in how power is exercised.

- *Power reveals the man.*

- *To know a man's principles, give him power.*

To be just and to defend one's own rights and those of others, which is our responsibility, requires fortitude.

– If you are going to have principles, you will need courage.

When an individual attempt to be just but lacks strength, it results in absurdity, as they will lack the firmness to act according to principles.

– Nothing is more ridiculous than someone pretending to be just while being weak.

When one has power but is weak, all sorts of deviations from justice will occur, leading to great harm.

– Fear the weak in power.

– Where fear rules, futility governs.

Fortitude and Prudence

Being prudent means having goals to achieve and results to defend, without which one cannot speak of fortitude or its components: courage, patience, perseverance, equanimity, or resignation.

– Without goals to achieve, there is no drive for fortitude.

– If men do not feel love, they have no drive for courage. (Lao Tzu)[313]

And without the discernment of what is good or bad to pursue the former and avoid the latter, fortitude degenerates into reckless boldness or temerity.

Audacity without judgment is destructive.

Prudence without fortitude is meaningless and degenerates into absurdity. To achieve goals and carry out resolutions, an individual needs to overcome numerous external and internal obstacles, repeatedly overcoming their inclinations and aversions, for which fortitude is necessary.

– To achieve lofty goals, you must be willing to pay the price.

Fortitude is also needed, particularly in the form of equanimity, to seek the proper mental state for reflection and decision-making.

– Let the mind calm and everything will be different.

– The answers you seek do not come when your mind is busy and agitated, but when it is clear and calm.

When an individual tries to be prudent but lacks strength, absurdity also arises, as they will lack the determination needed to fight for their goals.

– There is no greater difficulty than lack of will. (Spain)[314]

From what has been seen so far, it can be said that fortitude and prudence form an indissoluble unity, as one cannot exist without the other.

– Audacity without judgment is dangerous, and judgment without audacity is useless.

Moderation, Prudence, Justice, and Fortitude

Since moderation allows one to stay in the middle between vicious extremes, its existence is evaluated through other moral qualities. It is necessary for fortitude, justice, and prudence to avoid falling into their vices by crossing the boundaries of virtue, so there will be a lack of moderation in any of the vices of the other cardinal virtues.

– Nothing in excess.

Only with the existence of the four cardinal virtues—prudence, justice, moderation, and fortitude—can it be said that an individual is capable of exercising proper selfgovernance, which is essential for governing others.

– Great is the king who governs himself well. (Desiderius Erasmus)[315]

– Imposing your will on others is a demonstration of ordinary strength. Imposing it on yourself is a testament to true power. (Lao Tzu)[316]

– Only he who commands himself, commands. (José Martí)[317]

– To master others, you must first know how to master yourself.

FINAL CONSIDERATIONS

Fortitude is necessary for justice to defend the rights that we are responsible for defending. It is necessary for prudence to overcome internal and external obstacles that arise on the path to achieving goals and to seek the appropriate mental state or the best possible mental state for reflection and decision-making. Without fortitude, justice degenerates into injustice and absurdity; and moderation and prudence into excess and imprudence, respectively.

Justice is necessary for fortitude so that self-control is exercised while respecting the rights of others and oneself. It is necessary for prudence to ensure that the goals towards which an individual directs their life and the means chosen to achieve them are correct from an ethical and moral standpoint, conceived within the framework of respecting the rights of others and oneself. Without justice, fortitude degenerates into cruelty, prudence into cunning and wickedness, and moderation into excess.

Moderation is necessary for fortitude, justice, and prudence to avoid their vicious extremes by crossing the boundaries of virtue. Without moderation, fortitude degenerates into weakness or rigidity; and justice and prudence into injustice and excess, respectively.

Prudence is necessary for fortitude to have worthy goals to fight for and to differentiate what is beneficial from what is not in the struggle to achieve them. It is necessary for justice to determine one's own and others' rights in certain circumstances and the best ways to assert one's rights while respecting those of others. Without prudence, fortitude degenerates into weakness or rigidity; and justice and moderation into injustice and excess, respectively.

~~~

Chapter 11. GENERAL CONSIDERATIONS ON THE CARDINAL VIRTUES

In this section, we review the main ideas presented in the work, which are offered beginning with guidance or exhortation, explained concisely, and ending with a proverb or saying.

1. **Strive for clarity regarding your objectives.** Knowing your goals will help you avoid confusion and make your actions more effective. *If you know what you want, you can make mistakes like everyone else, but you'll make fewer.*

2. **Set achievable goals.** There are no effective procedures to achieve unattainable goals, and they are unattainable because the means you have or can have are insufficient and ineffective. Pursuing them will make you feel frustrated. *If you know you won't reach the goal, don't start.*

3. **Difficult does not mean impossible.** It is important to differentiate between unattainable goals and difficult yet achievable ones. *Difficult only means you have to think and work a little harder.*

4. **The path to your happiness lies in serving others.** Your goals should benefit others, which allows you to feel useful, and this is essential for happiness. *By seeking the good of others, we find our own.*

5. **Work towards your goals, but do not exhaust yourself doing so.** Even in objectives that greatly benefit others, avoid wearing yourself out with excessive dedication. *The overly tightened string breaks. (San Salvador)*[318]

6. **Avoid goals that harm you.** There are goals that, despite appearing attractive, will not lead to personal fulfillment but instead function as miscalculations in the pursuit of happiness, causing you harm and pain. Stay away from them. *There are ways that seem right to a man, but in the end, they lead to death.*

7. **Choose means that truly allow you to achieve your goals.** If the means you choose do not guarantee the achievement of your goals, you are destined to fail. *With an egg, you cannot break a rock.*

8. **The means used should allow for a positive cost-benefit ratio.** Ensure that the results you obtain correspond with the efforts you must make to achieve your goals. *If I lose more than I gain, what do I gain?*

9. **Choose means you will not regret later.** If the means you choose allow you to achieve your goals but later bring regret, they are not worth it. *Do not seek good ends by vile means.*

10. **Avoid unnecessary hesitations when choosing means.** The search for the best means should not degenerate into unproductive hesitations that paralyze you and prevent you from achieving your goals. *You can't make an omelet without breaking eggs.*

11. **Do not be deceived by appearances.** Very often, what seems harmful is beneficial, and what appears beneficial is harmful, so you must look beyond appearances. *There are ills that come for good, and for bad, not a few goods.*

12. **Establish priorities among your goals.** Since achieving certain goals can slow down or exclude the achievement of others, you must establish priorities among them to organize your actions. *Good decisions cannot come from bad priorities.*

13. **Act with timeliness.** If you act before circumstances are favorable, you will be ineffective and may ruin everything, and if you act afterward, you will have acted in vain. *In timeliness lies triumph.*

14. **Discretion is a weapon of protection.** Despite how friendly and harmless circumstances may appear, be discreet with information you know you should not reveal. *Your friend has a friend, and your friend's friend has another friend; therefore, be discreet.*

15. **Hide your projects.** Be careful when sharing your happiness or your plans, as this can provoke the pride of others and arouse destructive envy. *From not keeping quiet about your happiness, envy is born.*

16. **Control your impulses, or they will control you.** If you are impulsive, you will be wasting your potential for self-control and distancing yourself from the life you want for yourself. *Do not act on the first impulse.*

17. **If you have secrets that must be closely guarded, avoid getting drunk.** What you would not do sober, you might do under the influence of alcohol, including revealing information that should be kept hidden. *When wine enters, secrets come out.*

18. **Learn to say "No" to yourself.** One of the greatest victories for a human being is to abstain from doing what they know they shouldn't, even if they have a strong desire to do it. *Conquer your desires and you will conquer the whole world.*

19. **Restrain your desires when they are excessive or inappropriate.** Sometimes, mental peace is lost due to intense desires that are not fulfilled. An effective way to regain inner peace is to mitigate them. *Clip the wings of your chickens and your hopes, and you will not have to chase after them.*

20. **When you don't feel like doing something necessary, get active.** If you know what you have to do but lack the desire, just start doing it, and the willpower will follow. *The first step won't take you where you want to go, but it will get you out of where you are.*

21. **Solve problems while they are still small.** Address issues early to avoid the complications that will arise if they grow. *Prevent disorder before it becomes overwhelming. (Lao Tzu* [319]

22. **Do what you must and fear no one.** If you act righteously, you can sleep with a clear conscience, and anyone who speaks ill of you will have to lie. *If you walk upright, there is no crooked shadow. (China)* [320]

23. **Even if your rights have been violated, respect the rights of others.** The transgressor also has rights that you must respect to avoid becoming a transgressor yourself and facing consequences for your excesses. *Others' faults do not justify your own.*

24. **Assert your rights, but respect those of others.** Mutual respect is fundamental for achieving good interpersonal relationships. *There is peace when everyone respects the rights of others.*

25. **Treat others as you would like to be treated.** When unsure how to act, a good guide is to use yourself as a reference and treat others as you would like to be treated. *Man is a mirror for man.*

26. **Give what you would like to receive.** The way others project themselves towards you will largely depend on how you project yourself towards them. If you want to receive good treatment and actions, you must start by offering them to others. *Treatment is a psychic boomerang.*

27. **Be firm in your resolutions, but change when necessary.** Review your decisions and maintain them if they are correct, but do not hesitate to change them when needed. *If your decision doesn't work: change it.*

28. **Know your weaknesses.** Knowing your weak points allows you to take the necessary measures to overcome them or to stay away from stimuli that can make you falter. *He who does not know his limitations fails.*

29. **Dare to take the first step.** Every new venture has its risks, but often the only way to know the outcome of our actions is by taking the risk. *He who does not venture does not cross the sea.*

30. **Dominated by fear, your life will become poorer each day.** If you do not face the fears you must confront, you will fail to achieve several important goals in your life, and your existence will become impoverished. *A cowardly man does not enter the palace.*

31. **Avoid unnecessary dangers.** There is no glory in facing unnecessary dangers; it is rather a sign of imprudence that can bring perfectly avoidable negative consequences. *He who seeks danger perishes in it.*

32. **Learn to wait wisely.** Enduring the discomforts of a necessary wait is a path that must be traveled to reap the fruits of triumph and joy. *Patience is bitter, but its fruits are sweet.*

33. **Respect the processes.** Everything has its process and its own evolutionary time that must be respected, or everything will be ruined. *What forces evolution destroys it.*

34. **Instead of fighting time, make use of it.** When eagerly awaiting something, avoid fighting against time. Instead of suffering by wishing it would pass faster, fill that time with activities that enrich your life and distract you from the discomfort of waiting. *There is a way to beat time, and that is by making use of it.*

35. **He who rushes loses.** If you rush into doing or saying something without consideration, your actions are likely to be misplaced and will distance you from your goals. *Haste is the father of failure.*

36. **Keep a cool head.** No matter how urgent the situation, maintain control of yourself and pay attention to your actions. *A cool head allows you to see what needs to be done, even in difficult circumstances.*

37. **When necessary, change.** If you are getting bad results but continue doing the same thing under similar circumstances, you will most likely continue to get the same bad results. *If what you are doing isn't working, try changing it.*

38. **Don't count your chickens before they hatch.** When success seems imminent, maintain the necessary precautions until the triumph is fully achieved to avoid relaxation that leads to defeat. *Don't confuse the nearness of victory with the victory itself.*

39. **Maintain discipline in prosperity.** Facing prosperity requires as much effort and difficulty as facing adversity because, in prosperity, people tend to lose the necessary discipline and precautions, and thus lose what they have gained. *If you slack in prosperity, you lose it.*

40. **Everything passes.** Your life is neither as bad nor as good as your worst or best days; it constantly oscillates. Both success and failure, joy and sorrow are temporary. *It never rained without stopping, nor stopped without raining.*

41. **To deliberate properly, calm yourself first.** When under the influence of very intense emotional states, give yourself time to calm down and

deliberate more rationally. *Avoid making permanent decisions based on temporary emotions.*

42. **Accept what you cannot or should not change.** Accept irreplaceable losses and rebuild your life from the new situation. *Knowing how to endure makes suffering less.*

43. **Instead of worrying, take action.** Work diligently to resolve your problems, doing what depends on you, and remain calm about the rest. *Do your diligence, and let God act as He will.*

44. **Don't waste the good by complaining about the bad.** Instead of complaining about your problems or what you don't yet have, be grateful for what you do have, as you won't have it forever because everything changes. *Be more grateful and complain less.*

~~~

GLOSSARIES

THEORY OF VIRTUE

Altruism: Selfless concern for the well-being of others, often seen as a virtue that involves acting for others' benefit, even at one's own expense.

Areté: Excellent quality of people or things that enables them to perform their functions effectively and achieve their purpose.

Authenticity: Quality of being genuine or true to oneself, essential for maintaining personal integrity and moral behavior.

Cardinal, Principal, or Fundamental Virtues: Foundational moral qualities essential for all other positive traits. Traditionally identified as prudence, justice, fortitude, and moderation, these virtues have been discussed since antiquity by figures like Plato and Saint Ambrose.

Character: Set of enduring traits that define an individual's personality and way of being, shaping their behavior and actions.

Compassion: A sympathetic awareness of others' suffering, coupled with a desire to alleviate it, considered a foundational virtue in many ethical systems.

Consequentialism: Ethical theory that judges the morality of an action based on its outcomes or consequences, determining rightness by the goodness of results.

Deontology: Ethical theory emphasizing duty and rules in moral decision-making, rather than consequences, often associated with philosopher Immanuel Kant.

Deviation: A departure from accepted norms or customs, leading to behavior that differs from what is typical or expected.

Empathy: Ability to understand and share another's feelings, seen as key to emotional intelligence and moral development.

Ethical Relativism: Belief that morality is not universal and that ethical truths depend on cultural, social, or personal circumstances.

Eudaimonia: Often translated as "flourishing" or "happiness," referring to the highest human good in Aristotelian ethics, where life is lived according to virtue.

Excellence: Superior quality or goodness that makes something or someone worthy of special appreciation and esteem.

Fairness: Quality of making judgments free from discrimination or dishonesty, seen as essential to justice.

Golden Mean: A characteristic of moral virtues that consists of occupying an intermediate position between vicious extremes, one by excess and the other by deficiency. Example: Courage between cowardice and recklessness.

Greatness: Elevation of spirit and moral excellence, indicating a person's ability to achieve remarkable things.

Honorability: State of deserving respect due to contributions to the common good or possessing strong moral qualities.

Humility: Quality of having a modest view of one's importance, often seen as a virtue countering pride and arrogance.

Immorality: Actions or words that are contrary to the customs of a particular time and place.

Integrity: Condition of possessing all necessary moral qualities, leading to consistency in values and actions.

Justice: Principle of fairness and moral equity, involving giving each individual their due based on merit or need.

Magnanimity: Greatness and elevation of spirit, involving a desire for great honors and worthiness of them, according to Aristotle.

Mediocrity: State of being of average quality or having little merit, often tending toward poor quality.

Moral Vice: Poor quality in the moral realm that hinders fulfilling societal roles and causes difficulty in social adaptation.

Moral Virtue: Excellent qualities of a person in the moral realm, enabling them to act with righteousness and integrity.

Morality: Conformity of actions or words with the customs of a particular time and place.

Responsibility: State of being accountable for something, often seen as a moral obligation to act correctly and ethically.

Teleology: Philosophical approach emphasizing purpose and goal-oriented processes, judging actions based on their outcomes.

Vice: Poor quality of things or people in performing their functions.

Virtue: The quality or ability of things to produce effects, indicating excellent performance and moral integrity.

Virtuosity: The skill and ease in overcoming difficulties, showing mastery and perfection in any art or technique.

Wisdom: The ability to think and act using knowledge, experience, understanding, and insight, enabling good judgment.

PRUDENCE

Anticipation: Ability to foresee and prepare for future events and needs.

Astuteness: Skill in achieving goals by cleverly avoiding deception or being deceptive when necessary.

Caution: Practice of preventing risk or harm by acting with care and prudence to avoid danger.

Circumspection: Quality of considering circumstances carefully and behaving appropriately, showing seriousness and decorum.

Consideration: Thoughtful attention given to something, ensuring it is handled with care and respect.

Craftiness: Ability to skillfully and cleverly manage tasks or situations.

Decision-Making: Process of selecting the best course of action from multiple alternatives, influenced by willpower.

Deliberation: Thorough examination of reasons and options before making a decision or judgment.

Discernment: Skill of distinguishing between different options or elements, recognizing subtle differences.

Discretion: Practice of using common sense and tact in speaking or acting, often marked by reserve and prudence.

Effectiveness: Capacity to achieve desired outcomes or produce the intended effect.

Efficiency: Ability to achieve goals using resources rationally, maximizing the cost-benefit ratio.

End: Ultimate goal or purpose for which an action is undertaken.

Erudition: Possession of extensive knowledge in various subjects, often reflected in learned and varied reading.

Excess: Lack of moderation, leading to disorder by exceeding limits.

Foolishness: Quality of acting without reason, often characterized by ignorance or stubbornness.

Foresight: Ability to plan and prepare for future needs or contingencies effectively.

Haste: Act of rushing into actions or decisions without proper thought, often lacking prudence.

Hesitation: State of uncertainty or indecision, marked by wavering or irresolution.

Immaturity: Developmental stage where an individual lacks the qualities needed for effective social functioning.

Imprudence: Failure to guide actions toward beneficial goals due to a lack of discernment between good and bad.

Impulsiveness: Tendency to act quickly without careful thought or consideration.

Indecision: Difficulty in making choices, often due to perplexity or irresolution.

Indiscretion: Lack of proper judgment or appropriateness, especially when sharing sensitive information.

Insight: Ability to understand situations clearly and quickly, often involving sharpness of thought.

Intelligence: Capability to solve problems and adapt to new circumstances effectively.

Irresponsibility: Tendency to make important decisions without careful deliberation or foresight.

Judgment: Ability to make wise decisions, reflecting prudence and good sense in action.

Maturity: State of possessing the necessary qualities to function effectively in one's social environment.

Meaning of Life: System of personal objectives that provides a sense of purpose and justification for one's existence.

Means: Resources or methods used to achieve a specific end or objective.

Method: Systematic approach to achieving a goal or resolving a problem.

Pragmatism: Practical approach to handling problems, emphasizing results and effective solutions.

Resourcefulness: Ability to find creative and effective solutions to challenges and obstacles.

Savvy: Practical knowledge and ability to handle situations efficiently and effectively.

Tact: Skill and sensitivity needed to navigate interpersonal relationships and difficult issues gracefully.

Vision: Ability to plan and envision the future with imagination and wisdom.

MODERATION

Abstinence: Ability to refrain, either completely or partially, from satisfying appetites when necessary.

Appetite: An impulse that drives the satisfaction of desires or needs.

Austerity: Quality of strictly adhering to moral norms and avoiding excess or indulgence.

Balance: State of maintaining equilibrium between different elements, avoiding extremes.

Composure: Ability to maintain calmness, modesty, and self-control in various situations.

Composure: State of being calm and in control of oneself, especially in difficult situations.

Containment: Act of restraining or moderating a passion or desire.

Contentment: The state of being satisfied with what one has, leading to a balanced and moderate outlook on life.

Continence: Moderation of passions or feelings, with the ability to refrain from actions that one desires but knows should not be done, and to defer actions to an appropriate time when circumstances require.

Decorum: Behavior in keeping with good taste and propriety, ensuring actions are appropriate and restrained.

Desire: Emotional longing or movement towards something that is wanted or needed.

Discipline: Practice of training oneself to act in accordance with rules and standards, promoting self-control and moderation.

Equanimity: Quality of maintaining calmness and composure under stress, allowing for balanced and rational actions.

Equilibrium: State of balance between opposing forces or actions, allowing for harmony and stability.

Eutrapelia: Virtue that moderates excessive amusements or entertainments, promoting urbanity and harmless wit.

Excess: Lack of moderation, leading to the violation of limits and resulting in disorder.

Frugality: Practice of being sparing or moderate in eating and drinking, often associated with simplicity.

Greed: Disordered desire for wealth or other possessions, marked by a lack of self-control.

Hatred: Intense aversion or antipathy towards someone or something, often accompanied by a desire to cause harm.

Immoderation: Absence of moderation, leading to excessive behavior or actions.

Impulse: Sudden desire or motive that prompts action without reflection.

Impulsiveness: Tendency to act or speak without reflection or caution, driven by momentary impulses.

Incontinence: Difficulty or inability to control emotional states or desires, often leading to inappropriate actions.

Intemperance: Inability to moderate appetites or desires, leading to excess.

Love: Deep feeling of affection and connection towards another person, characterized by a desire for mutual fulfillment and companionship.

Moderation: Ability to avoid both excesses and deficiencies, preventing the violation of limits that can harm oneself or others.

Nonsense: Actions or words that lack reason, sense, or appropriateness.

Objective: Mental anticipation of a desired result towards which activity is directed.

Opportunity: Timeliness and appropriateness of actions in a particular time and place, indicating a sense of occasion.

Passion: Strong emotion or desire, often leading to intense feelings and actions.

Patience: Ability to wait calmly and endure difficult situations without becoming agitated or upset.

Premeditation: Act of thinking reflectively about something before taking action.

Prevention: Act of anticipating and preparing to avoid risks or difficulties in achieving an objective.

Prudence: Ability to make sound decisions and judgments, guiding life towards good objectives through appropriate means.

Reflection: Process of careful and thoughtful consideration of a matter before making a decision.

Resolution: Determination and courage to act decisively and effectively.

Responsibility: Ability to show care and attention in decisions and actions, fulfilling obligations to oneself and others.

Restraint: Act of controlling or suppressing excessive force or emotions.

Rigorism: Excessive severity in moral or disciplinary matters, often leading to harshness.

Sagacity: Ability to foresee and prevent problems through wisdom and insight.

Sanity: State of having good judgment and prudence, leading to rational and balanced actions.

Self-Control: Ability to regulate one's emotions, thoughts, and behaviors in the face of temptations and impulses.

Serenity: Quality of being calm and peaceful, free from disturbance.

Sobriety: Practice of moderation and temperance, avoiding excessive adornments or behavior.

Stolidity: Total lack of sensitivity or awareness, often leading to unreasonable behavior.

Tact: Ability to handle delicate matters with sensitivity and prudence.

Temperance: Moderation of appetites and desires, subjecting them to reason and control.

Temptation: Stimulus that induces the desire for something, often leading to moral challenges.

Thoughtlessness: Quality of being imprudent and lacking common sense, leading to hasty actions.

Unrestrainedness: Tendency to act according to one's inclinations without regard for order or reason.

Untimeliness: Lack of appropriateness in timing, leading to actions that are out of place or time.

Whim: Arbitrary decision inspired by a sudden mood or desire for something extravagant.

Will: Faculty of deciding and directing one's behavior, involving the selection and prioritization of motives.

Wisdom: Combination of prudence and good judgment, enabling sound decision-making.

JUSTICE

Accountability: Obligation to take responsibility for one's actions, ensuring transparency and fairness.

Aggressiveness: Tendency to act or respond with violence or combativeness.

Anomie: State of society characterized by a breakdown or absence of social norms and values.

Arbitrariness: Actions or decisions made contrary to justice, reason, or laws, often based on personal will or whim.

Assertiveness: Ability to express one's rights, feelings, needs, and viewpoints confidently and respectfully without infringing on the rights of others.

Austerity: Practice of strictly adhering to moral norms and maintaining discipline in behavior.

Balance: State of fairness in distributing rights and responsibilities, ensuring equality.

Commutative Justice: Principle of giving each person what they are due, based on a fair exchange or proportionality in transactions.

Diplomacy: Practice of managing relations and resolving conflicts with tact and fairness, ensuring peaceful outcomes.

Distributive Justice: Principle of distributing resources and benefits fairly to reduce inequalities, focusing on supporting the weakest members of society.

Duty: Moral obligation to act in a specific manner, often guided by ethics and responsibility.

Equality: State of being equal, ensuring that everyone receives the same treatment and opportunities.

Equity: Practice of fairness and benevolent moderation, guided by conscience and the principle of giving each person what they deserve.

Eunomia: Ideal of proper order and balance in society and individuals, emphasizing moderation and avoiding excess.

Fairness: Quality of making impartial judgments that are free from discrimination, ensuring equitable treatment for all.

Honesty: Quality of being truthful and acting with integrity in all actions.

Impartiality: Ability to apply justice without bias or favoritism, ensuring fairness in decisions and actions.

Infamy: State of dishonor or disgrace due to wickedness or vile actions.

Iniquity: State of great injustice or wickedness, often characterized by unfair actions.

Injustice: Actions or habits that violate the rights of others or fail to fulfill one's duties, leading to unfair treatment.

Integrity: Quality of being upright and fair in the administration of justice, maintaining discipline and firmness of spirit.

Justice: Quality of giving each person what is rightfully theirs, including fairness to oneself.

Laxity: Excessive weakness or leniency in applying justice or asserting rights.

Legality: Adherence to laws and regulations, ensuring truthful and upright behavior in fulfilling responsibilities.

Leniency: Tendency to be gentle or forgiving in enforcing duties or administering punishment.

Liberty: Freedom to act according to one's rights without infringing on others' rights, ensuring justice and fairness.

Morality: System of principles and values that guide ethical behavior and decision-making.

Neutrality: Practice of remaining impartial and fair in conflicts, guided solely by justice.

Partiality: Biased inclination for or against someone or something, leading to unfair judgment or actions.

Passivity: Quality of allowing others to violate rights without taking action, often resulting in insufficient defense of justice.

Perversity: Intention to cause harm and disrupt order, leading to corruption and injustice.

Rectitude: Quality of being fair and firm in decisions, ensuring impartiality and justice.

Respect: Acknowledgment and esteem given to individuals based on their rights and dignity.

Right: Recognition of a benefit or freedom that is protected morally or legally.

Rigor: Strictness and precision in applying justice, ensuring fairness and adherence to rules.

Sensitivity: Ability to understand and empathize with others' perspectives, recognizing their feelings and needs.

Severity: Harshness and strictness in administering justice or punishment, often lacking leniency.

Tolerance: Willingness to accept and respect different views, beliefs, and practices without bias.

Vengeance: Act of seeking retribution, often contrary to the principles of justice and fairness.

Wickedness: Quality of being evil or unjust, often leading to unfair treatment and harm.

FORTITUDE

Bravery: Quality of facing danger, pain, or adversity with courage and without fear.

Cowardice: Inability to overcome fear when necessary, or a lack of skill to act courageously in difficult situations.

Determination: Firmness of purpose and the ability to pursue goals with persistence and resolve.

Endurance: Ability to withstand hardship or adversity over time, showing patience and resilience.

Firmness: Strength of spirit to maintain justice and discipline, showing resolute determination.

Flexibility: Ability to adapt and redirect efforts to achieve goals, showing openness to change.

Fortitude: Strength to maintain resolutions and persevere despite internal and external pressures, acting appropriately in challenging circumstances.

Fragility: Quality of being easily broken or weakened, often leading to vulnerability and susceptibility to vice.

Hesitation: State of wavering or feeling uncertain, often leading to indecision or vacillation in choices and actions.

Immutability: Quality of being unchanging and resistant to emotional reactions, showing stability but lacking adaptability.

Inadaptability: Inability to adjust or adapt to new situations or environments, leading to challenges in flexibility.

Inconsistency: Lack of stability, solidity, or coherence in behavior and decisions.

Indecision: Difficulty in making choices or decisions, often due to perplexity or irresolution.

Indetermination: Absence of determination or resolution, leading to a lack of decisive action.

Inflexibility: Lack of self-regulation and adaptability, leading to rigid adherence to outdated norms that hinder progress.

Invariability: Quality of being unchanging or resistant to change, often resulting in stagnation.

Irresolution: State of being unable to make firm decisions, leading to indecisiveness.

Languor: Lack of strength, energy, or spirit, often resulting in weakness and lethargy.

Laxity: Excessive softness or weakness in enforcing justice or claiming rights, leading to a lack of firmness.

Obstacle: Hindrance or impediment that challenges progress or achievement, often requiring fortitude to overcome.

Pusillanimity: Lack of courage to face misfortunes or take on significant challenges, often marked by faintheartedness.

Rectitude: Quality of being morally correct and firm in resolutions, ensuring just and fair actions.

Resilience: Capacity to recover quickly from difficulties and adapt to challenging circumstances.

Resolution: Determination and courage to make decisive decisions and act with valor and promptness.

Rigidity: Quality of being overly strict and inflexible, often hindering change and adaptation.

Rigorism: Excessive strictness or severity in moral or disciplinary matters, lacking compassion or flexibility.

Self-Confidence: Belief in one's abilities and resources to face life's demands successfully.

Self-Insecurity: Belief that one lacks the necessary resources and abilities to handle life's challenges.

Severity: Quality of being harsh and strict in treatment or punishment, showing little leniency.

Shortcoming: Deficiency in talent, resolution, or ability, often leading to timidity or lack of confidence.

Stiffness: Quality of being rigid and inflexible, often resulting in excessive seriousness or affectation.

Stoicism: Endurance of pain or hardship without complaint, reflecting strength and fortitude.

Strictness: Adherence to rules or laws without interpretation, showing a firm and uncompromising stance.

Timidity: Social behavior marked by inhibitions and fears in the presence of others, often leading to a lack of assertiveness.

Weakness: Lack of energy or vigor in spirit and resolutions, making it difficult to overcome temptations or challenges.

COURAGE

Bravery: Quality of displaying effort and courage in facing challenges and adversity.

Chutzpah: Audacity and confidence to face difficult situations boldly and without hesitation.

Courage: Ability to confront and overcome fear in the appropriate manner, place, and time when necessary.

Cowardice: Inability to overcome fear when required, or the lack of skill to do so in challenging circumstances.

Daring: Willingness to take risks or face danger with confidence and boldness.

Escapism: Tendency to evade reality and avoid confronting problems or conflicts that need to be faced.

Evasion: Act of avoiding difficulty, harm, or danger through cunning or artfulness, often neglecting responsibilities.

Evasiveness: Propensity to avoid dangers or difficulties, often by neglecting them rather than addressing them.

Fear: Emotional state that arises when an individual perceives the possibility of harm, whether rightly or wrongly.

Grit: Determination and perseverance to overcome obstacles and continue striving towards goals despite challenges.

Heroism: Conduct of a hero, showing remarkable bravery and courage in the face of adversity.

Intrepidity: Quality of being bold and brave in facing dangers, showing courage and fearlessness.

Pluck: Courage and determination to face challenges or adversity with confidence and boldness.

Rashness: Tendency to expose oneself to unnecessary dangers or risks without proper consideration, often seen as imprudent boldness.

Resolve: Firm determination to face challenges and difficulties with courage and persistence.

Spunk: Courage and determination to face challenges with spirit and resilience.

PATIENCE

Acceptance: Willingness to tolerate or accept situations, people, or conditions, demonstrating patience and understanding.

Calmness: State of being peaceful and free from disturbance, often associated with patience and tranquility.

Composure: Ability to remain calm and self-controlled, even under stress or pressure.

Composure: State of being calm and in control of oneself, especially in stressful situations.

Despair: State of mind where hope has faded because what is desired seems impossible to achieve.

Endurance: Strength or vigor to withstand pressures, challenges, and difficulties, demonstrating resilience and persistence.

Haste: Urgency and speed with which something is done, often driven by the need or desire to act quickly.

Hope: State of mind where what is desired appears possible and attainable, providing motivation and optimism.

Impatience: Inability to wait patiently during necessary delays, characterized by a lack of self-control and "not knowing how to wait."

Imperturbability: Ability to maintain calmness and composure in the face of disturbances, showing emotional stability.

Inopportuneness: Acting at an inappropriate time, place, or purpose, often leading to unfavorable outcomes.

Intolerance: Lack of ability to endure and accept differences or annoying characteristics of others, resulting in impatience and non-acceptance.

Longanimity: Greatness and constancy of spirit during long-lasting adversities, showing benevolence and patience.

Moment: Suitable opportunity or occasion for action, where timing is key to success.

Obstinacy: Inability to let go of goals or plans involving a wait, despite their impracticality or senselessness.

Passivity: Quality of enduring unfavorable circumstances and irritating characteristics of others without taking action, often reflecting patience or tolerance.

Patience: Ability to endure suffering and discomfort during necessary waits, demonstrating self-control and perseverance.

Precipitation: Act of hastily doing or saying something without consideration, often leading to mistakes.

Resilience: Capacity to recover quickly from difficulties, demonstrating strength and patience.

Serenity: Quality of being calm, peaceful, and untroubled, reflecting inner peace and patience.

Stoicism: Endurance of pain or hardship without complaint, showing fortitude and patience.

Timeliness: Appropriateness of time and place for an action, ensuring the best outcome.

Tolerance: Ability to endure and accept situations or characteristics of others that may be irritating, reflecting respect and acceptance of differences.

PERSEVERANCE

Application: Diligence and fondness with which something is done, especially in studying or learning.

Assiduity: Consistent and frequent dedication to a task, demonstrating punctuality and constant effort.

Constancy: Firmness and perseverance of spirit in maintaining resolutions and purposes over time.

Contumacy: Stubbornness and tenacity in holding onto an error or mistaken belief.

Determination: Decisiveness and perseverance in executing a plan or goal, showing strong willpower.

Doggedness: Quality of being determined and persistent in the face of adversity, often refusing to give up.

Endurance: Capacity to withstand hardship or adversity over time, showing patience and perseverance.

Firmness: Stability and steadiness of someone who remains unmoved or unwavered by challenges.

Flexibility: Ability to adapt and reorient activities and objectives when necessary, ensuring progress towards goals.

Grit: Strength of character that involves courage, resolve, and determination in facing adversity.

Immutability: Quality of being unchangeable and resistant to alteration, often reflecting stability but lacking adaptability.

Inadaptability: Inability to adjust or adapt to new situations or changes, leading to challenges in flexibility.

Inconsistency: Lack of consistency, stability, or solidity in actions, thoughts, or decisions.

Inconstancy: Tendency to change opinions, thoughts, or commitments easily, showing a lack of firmness and stability.

Inflexibility: Lack of adaptability and self-regulation, often leading to rigid adherence to outdated norms or practices.

Lack of Application: Absence of effort, diligence, and interest in pursuing a task or goal.

Listlessness: Lack of enthusiasm, energy, or interest in an activity, often leading to tedium or boredom.

Negligence: Carelessness and lack of diligence in fulfilling duties or responsibilities.

Obfuscation: State of being stubbornly confused or unclear, often persisting in misunderstanding.

Obstacle: Impediment or difficulty that hinders progress and requires perseverance to overcome.

Obstinacy: Inability to reconsider or abandon goals despite their irrationality or impracticality.

Perseverance: Firmness in maintaining purposes despite internal and external obstacles, showing continued effort and resilience.

Persistence: Continued effort to achieve a goal despite obstacles, maintaining a steady and unwavering course.

Pertinacity: Stubbornness or tenacity in holding onto an opinion, doctrine, or resolution, often without flexibility.

Resolution: Firm determination to pursue goals with steadfastness and tenacity.

Rigidity: Extreme severity and inflexibility in thoughts and actions, making change difficult.

Stubbornness: Quality of being irreducible in thought, feeling, and action, often leading to persistence without reason.

Tenacity: Quality of being difficult to separate from a goal or belief, offering strong resistance to challenges.

Versatility: Ability to adapt easily and quickly to various tasks and situations, showing flexibility and resourcefulness.

Weakness: Lack of strength or vigor to resist challenges, often leading to susceptibility in opinions and decisions.

Willpower: Ability to control impulses and make decisions that align with long-term goals, showing mental strength.

EQUANIMITY

Adversity: Situation of misfortune or hardship in which a person finds themselves, often requiring resilience and equanimity.

Affectivity: Psychological expression of moods, emotions, and feelings, reflecting the quality of experience in relation to biological and social needs.

Apathy: Lack of emotion, vigor, or interest, characterized by indifference and insensitivity to stimuli or events.

Balance: Ability to maintain equilibrium and stability in thoughts and emotions, ensuring consistency in actions.

Calm: State of stillness and tranquility, marked by serenity and peace of mind.

Catatimia: Distortion of subjective perception of reality caused by emotional influence, leading to skewed judgment.

Composure: Ability to maintain gravity, serenity, and circumspection, especially in stressful situations.

Composure: Quality of maintaining calmness and control, even under stress or pressure.

Contentment: State of being satisfied with what one has, reflecting a balanced and equanimous outlook on life.

Dejection: State of pessimism and reduced initiative, often accompanied by a lack of spirit or motivation.

Detachment: Ability to separate oneself emotionally from situations, maintaining objectivity and equanimity.

Equanimity: Quality of maintaining calmness, constancy, and impartiality of judgment in the face of changing fortunes or circumstances.

Failure: Adverse outcome or the inability to achieve a desired goal or result, often requiring resilience to overcome.

Fortune: Sequence of fortuitous events that can influence outcomes positively or negatively.

Frustration: Feeling of dissatisfaction when a goal-oriented behavior is blocked by obstacles, leading to emotional distress.

Impassibility: Inability to feel or suffer, characterized by emotional detachment and indifference.

Imperturbability: Ability to remain calm and unperturbed, regardless of external disturbances.

Impulsivity: Tendency to act or speak without reflection or caution, driven by momentary impulses.

Incontinence: Difficulty or inability to control emotional states, leading to challenges in self-control.

Intrepidity: Quality of being bold, courageous, and serene in the face of danger or adversity.

Joy: Pleasant emotional state characterized by feelings of satisfaction and well-being, often resulting from success or achievement.

Lightness: Ease with which thoughts and emotions change, often reflecting a lack of seriousness or consistency.

Mindfulness: Practice of being present and aware of one's thoughts and emotions, promoting equanimity and clarity.

Prosperity: Favorable course of events leading to success and well-being in one's endeavors.

Sadness: Unpleasant emotional state characterized by discomfort and dissatisfaction, often arising from loss or failure.

Serenity: Calm and peaceful state without physical or moral disturbance, reflecting inner peace and tranquility.

Steadfastness: Quality of being resolute and unwavering, showing consistency and determination in one's actions.

Stoicism: Practice of maintaining fortitude and control over one's sensitivity, showing equanimity in the face of adversity.

Success: Achievement of a desired goal or outcome, resulting in satisfaction and fulfillment.

Tranquility: State of peace and calm, free from disturbance or agitation, often associated with equanimity.

Variability: Tendency to change or be changeable, often reflecting instability or inconstancy.

RESIGNATION

Acceptance: Act of acknowledging a situation or condition without resistance, showing willingness to face reality.

Accommodation: Process of adjusting to new circumstances or requirements, demonstrating flexibility and adaptability.

Adaptability: Ability to make necessary changes and adjustments in response to changing circumstances.

Complacency: Tendency to be satisfied with the status quo, often leading to a lack of motivation to improve or change.

Complaining: Habit of expressing dissatisfaction or grievances frequently, often without significant reason.

Conformism: Acceptance and compliance with situations or conditions that could be changed for improvement, often due to unwillingness to act.

Conformity: Acceptance of misfortune or adversity without attempting to change the situation, often seen as passive acceptance.

Endurance: Ability to withstand hardship or adversity with patience and perseverance, demonstrating resilience and strength.

Inadaptability: Inability to adjust or adapt to new situations, leading to challenges in response to change.

Inconformity: Tendency to resist or oppose the established order in political, social, moral, or aesthetic matters.

Passivity: Tendency to endure unfavorable influences from the environment or actions of others without taking sufficient action. ‖ 2. Allowing others to act without participating or intervening oneself.

Relinquishment: Act of giving up or surrendering control or possession, often showing acceptance and letting go.

Resignation: Acceptance and compliance with situations that cannot or should not be changed, demonstrating patience and acceptance.

Submission: Act of accepting the authority or will of another, often showing compliance without resistance.

Tolerance: Willingness to endure difficult situations or the beliefs and behaviors of others, even if they are different from one's own.

Yielding: Act of giving in or surrendering to a situation or condition, often showing compliance and acceptance.

***~~~**

BIBLIOGRAPHIC REFERENCES AND NOTES

1 Aristotle. Virtues and Vices. Discusiones Filosóficas. 2009;10(14):133-45. Available from: http://www.scielo.org.co/scielo.php?script=sci_arttext&pid=S0124-61272009000100009&lng=en&tlng=es

2 Abbagnano, N. Dictionary of Philosophy. Havana, Cuba: Cuban Institute of the Book; 1972. Aretology; p. 97.

3 Fowers BJ, Cokelet B, Leonhardt ND. Virtue Theory. In: The Science of Virtue: A Framework for Research. Cambridge: Cambridge University Press; 2024. p. 25-52. Available from: https://doi.org/10.1017/9781108779968.003

4 Iovchuk, M. T., Oizerman, T. I., & Shchipanov, I. Y. History of Philosophy. Vol. I. Third Edition. Moscow: Progress Publishers; 1978. p. 54.

5 Aristotle. Nicomachean Ethics and Politics. Mexico: Editorial Porrúa, S.A.; 1992. p. 22.

6 Aristotle. Nicomachean Ethics and Politics. Mexico: Editorial Porrúa, S.A.; 1992. pp. 18-27, 23, 26.

7 Aristotle emphasizes in almost every book of his Nicomachean Ethics, especially in Books III and V, the importance of the voluntariness of an act for it to be morally evaluable. (Aristotle. Nicomachean Ethics and Politics. Mexico: Editorial Porrúa, S.A., 1992; p. 22).

8 Aristotle. Nicomachean Ethics and Politics. Mexico: Editorial Porrúa, S.A.; 1992. pp. 18-27.

9 Thinkers like Hugo Grotius (1585–1645) criticize Aristotle for suggesting that justice lies between vicious extremes (The Internet Encyclopedia of Philosophy. Virtue Theory. Internet, 1996). However, this is an incorrect interpretation of the Stagirite's doctrine, as he posits that there is a complete justice in which injustice is the only vice. Additionally, there is a particular injustice that arises from the existence of a specific vice for which extremes do exist. (Aristotle. Nicomachean Ethics and Politics. Mexico: Editorial Porrúa, S.A.; 1992. p. 60).

10 Diogenes L. Lives of the Eminent Philosophers. Barcelona: Orbis; 1985; Vol. II, pp. 67-68.

11 Cortés Morató, J., & Martínez Riu, A. Dictionary of Philosophy [CD-ROM]. Barcelona, Spain: Empresa Editorial Herder S.A.; Ambrosio; 1996.

12 Abbagnano, N. Dictionary of Philosophy. Havana, Cuba: Cuban Institute of the Book; 1972. Cardinal Virtues; p. 144.

13 Vidal, M. Dictionary of Theological Ethics. Navarra, Spain: Editorial Verbo Divino; 1991. pp. 631-633.

14 There are important similarities and differences between the Theory of Values or Axiology and the Theory of Virtue or Aretology. One of the similarities is that both focus on the problem of human behavior and the psychological elements that precede it, in terms of "what is right" to follow and "what is wrong" to avoid or reject, establishing a hierarchy and order of priorities among human qualities, both positive and negative. Both theories propose a model of the human being to be achieved. A significant point of differentiation between the two is the relationship between the concepts of moral virtue and ethical-moral value. The former has been defined as the excellent qualities of a person in the moral realm, while the latter is nothing more than the positive significance of those excellent qualities, both for society and for the individual who possesses them. These are not parallel or alternative theories; rather, the Theory of Moral Virtues is part of the historical trajectory of ethical-moral axiology.

15 Those notes were first published in a work titled Machiavelli Commented by Napoleon, edited in Paris in 1816 by Abbot Silvestre Guillon. (Machiavelli, N. The Prince. Argentina: Editorial Sopena; 1955).

16 The Quran. In: Pérez Betancourt, A., et al. Error Hunting. Havana, Cuba: Editorial Ciencias Sociales; 1990. p. 54.

17 It's not about erudition or deep knowledge in a specific field. There are plenty of examples of those who possess such knowledge yet have serious difficulties managing themselves.

18 Sánchez Hernández, A. J. Ethical-Moral Values from a Psychological Perspective. Revista Humanidades Médicas, Vol. 6, No. 18, September - December 2006.

19 Confucius in: Lin Yutang. The Wisdom of Confucius. Buenos Aires, Argentina: Ediciones Siglo Veinte; 1952. p. 121.

20 Martí, J. Complete Works. Vol. II. Commemorative Edition of the 50th Anniversary of His Death. Havana, Cuba: Editorial Lex; 1946. p. 1843.

21 Confucius in: Lin Yutang. The Wisdom of Confucius. Buenos Aires, Argentina: Ediciones Siglo Veinte; 1952. p. 138.

22 Valdés Jane, E. Divinatory Sayings of the Shell and the Odun of Ifá - In Cuban Santería - Documents for the History and Culture of Osha-Ifá in Cuba. Proverbs from (4-12) Iroso tonti Eyilá. First Edition: Proyecto Orunmila; 2007. p. 16. https://www.academia.edu/8122356/Libro_de_Refranes_De_Diloggun_e_Ifa

23 Valdés Jane, E. *Divinatory Sayings of the Shell and the Odun of Ifá - In Cuban Santería - Documents for the History and Culture of Osha-Ifá in Cuba. Sayings from (11-14) Ojuani tonti Merinlá. First Edition: Proyecto Orunmila; 2007. p. 48. https://www.academia.edu/8122356/Libro_de_Refranes_De_Diloggun_e_Ifa*

24 Valdés Jane, E. *Divinatory Sayings of the Shell and the Odun of Ifá - In Cuban Santería - Documents for the History and Culture of Osha-Ifá in Cuba. Sayings from (8-1) Eyeúnle tonti Okana. First Edition: Proyecto Orunmila; 2007. p. 29. https://www.academia.edu/8122356/Libro_de_Refranes_De_Diloggun_e_Ifa*

25 Martí, J. *Complete Works. Vol. II. Commemorative Edition of the 50th Anniversary of His Death. Havana, Cuba: Editorial Lex; 1946. p. 1855.*

26 Tagore's quote is: *"I slept and dreamed that life was joy, I awoke and saw that life was service, I served and saw that service was joy." Tagore Rabindranath. Wikiquote. Free collection of quotes and famous sayings. https://es.wikiquote.org/wiki/Rabindranath_Tagore*

27 Martí, J. *Our America III. School of Arts and Crafts. In: Complete Works, Vol. VIII. Havana, Cuba: Editorial de Ciencias Sociales; 1991. p. 285.*

28 Feijóo, S. *From Flattery to Wisecrack: Oral Folklore of Cuba. Havana, Cuba: Editorial Letras Cubanas; 1981. p. 32.*

29 Solís, José A. *Sayings, Proverbs, Phrases, and Sentences: All the Treasure of Popular Wisdom of the Peoples of Spain at Your Fingertips. Spain: El Arca de Papel Editores; 2003. p. 116.*

30 United Bible Societies. *God Speaks Today. The Bible with Deuterocanonical Books. Old Testament. Proverbs. Popular Version. Second Edition. Mexico City: United Bible Societies; 1987. pp. 590, 593.*

31 *Work addiction constitutes a vicious extreme of industriousness, which is often not recognized as a negative quality to avoid.*

32 Solís, José A. *Sayings, Proverbs, Phrases, and Sentences: All the Treasure of Popular Wisdom of the Peoples of Spain at Your Fingertips. La Coruña, Spain: El Arca de Papel Editores; 2003. p. 153.*

33 Feijóo, S. *The Knowledge of Juan Without Anything: Signs in the Expression of the Peoples. Saying. Santa Clara, Cuba: Revista Signos. No. 14. Year 5, No. 2; January-April 1974. p. 105.*

34 Solís, José A. *Sayings, Proverbs, Phrases, and Sentences: All the Treasure of Popular Wisdom of the Peoples of Spain at Your Fingertips. La Coruña, Spain: El Arca de Papel Editores; 2003. p. 105.*

35 Solís, José A. *Sayings, Proverbs, Phrases, and Sentences: All the Treasure of Popular Wisdom of the Peoples of Spain at Your Fingertips. La Coruña, Spain: El Arca de Papel Editores; 2003. p. 106.*

36 Solís, José A. *Sayings, Proverbs, Phrases, and Sentences: All the Treasure of Popular Wisdom of the Peoples of Spain at Your Fingertips. La Coruña, Spain: El Arca de Papel Editores; 2003. p. 134.*

37 Feijóo, S. *The Knowledge of Juan Without Anything: Signs in the Expression of the Peoples. Saying. Santa Clara, Cuba: Revista Signos. No. 14. Year 5, No. 2; January-April 1974. p. 159.*

38 Feijóo, S. *The Knowledge of Juan Without Anything: Signs in the Expression of the Peoples. Saying. Santa Clara, Cuba: Revista Signos. No. 14. Year 5, No. 2; January-April 1974. p. 87.*

39 Valdés Jane, E. *Divinatory Sayings of the Shell and the Odun of Ifá - In Cuban Santería - Documents for the History and Culture of Osha-Ifá in Cuba. Sayings from (13-7) Metanlá tonti Odí. First Edition: Proyecto Orunmila; 2007. p. 55. Available at URL: https://www.academia.edu/8122356/Libro_de_Refranes_De_Diloggun_e_Ifa*

40 Feijóo, S. *The Knowledge of Juan Without Anything: Signs in the Expression of the Peoples. Saying. Santa Clara, Cuba: Revista Signos. No. 14. Year 5, No. 2; January-April 1974. p. 200.*

41 Feijóo, S. *The Knowledge of Juan Without Anything: Signs in the Expression of the Peoples. Saying. Santa Clara, Cuba: Revista Signos. No. 14. Year 5, No. 2; January-April 1974. p. 199.*

42 Flores-Huerta, S. *Sayings or Proverbs: Thematic Compendium. Mexico: CopIt-arXives; 2016. p. 35. Available at: http://scifunam.fisica.unam.mx/mir/copit/CD0006ES/CD0006ES.pdf*

43 United Bible Societies. *God Speaks Today. The Bible with Deuterocanonical Books. Deuterocanonical Books. Sirach. Popular Version. Second Edition. Mexico City: United Bible Societies; 1987. p. 97.*

44 Flores-Huerta, S. *Sayings or Proverbs: Thematic Compendium. Mexico: CopIt-arXives; 2016. p. 30. Available at: http://scifunam.fisica.unam.mx/mir/copit/CD0006ES/CD0006ES.pdf*

45 Flores-Huerta, S. *Sayings or Proverbs: Thematic Compendium. Mexico: CopIt-arXives; 2016. p. 30. Available at: http://scifunam.fisica.unam.mx/mir/copit/CD0006ES/CD0006ES.pdf*

46 Feijóo, S. *From Flattery to Wisecrack: Oral Folklore of Cuba. Havana, Cuba: Editorial Letras Cubanas; 1981. p. 27.*

47 Solís, José A. *Sayings, Proverbs, Phrases, and Sentences: All the Treasure of Popular Wisdom of the Peoples of Spain at Your Fingertips.* Spain: El Arca de Papel Editores; 2003. p. 20.

48 Cicero. *Cited in: Sintes Pros, J. Great Dictionary of Famous Quotes.* Barcelona, Spain: Editorial Sintes; 1960. p. 151.

49 Valdés Jane, E. *Divinatory Sayings of the Shell and the Odun of Ifá - In Cuban Santería - Documents for the History and Culture of Osha-Ifá in Cuba. Sayings from (4-10) Iroso tonti Ofún.* First Edition: Proyecto Orunmila; 2007. p. 15. Available at: *https://www.academia.edu/8122356/Libro_de_Refranes_De_Diloggun_e_Ifa*

50 Latin Proverb: *Pelle sub-agnina latitat mens saepe lupina. Feijóo, S. The Knowledge of Juan Without Anything: Signs in the Expression of the Peoples. Saying.* Santa Clara, Cuba: Revista Signos. No. 14. Year 5, No. 2; January-April 1974. p. 18.

51 Feijóo S. *The Knowledge of Juan Sin Nada. Signs in the Expression of the People. Sayings.* Santa Clara, Cuba. Signos Magazine. No. 14. Year 5, No. 2; January-April 1974. p. 67.

52 Feijóo S. *The Knowledge of Juan Sin Nada. Signs in the Expression of the People. Sayings.* Santa Clara, Cuba. Signos Magazine. No. 14. Year 5, No. 2; January-April 1974, p. 130.

53 Feijóo S. *The Knowledge of Juan Sin Nada. Signs in the Expression of the People. Sayings.* Santa Clara, Cuba. Signos Magazine. No. 14. Year 5, No. 2; January-April 1974. p. 195.

54 Feijóo S. *The Knowledge of Juan Without Anything: Signs in the Expression of the People. Sayings.* Santa Clara, Cuba. Signos Magazine. No. 14. Year 5, No. 2; January-April 1974. p. 98.

55 Vishnu Sarma. *Panchatantra.* Havana, Cuba: Editorial Arte y Literatura; 1989, p. 213.

56 Feijóo S. *From Compliments to Sayings: Oral Folklore of Cuba.* Havana, Cuba: Editorial Letras Cubanas; 1981. p. 19.

57 Sintes Pros J. *Dictionary of Aphorisms, Proverbs, and Sayings.* Barcelona, Spain: Editorial Sintes; 1954. pp. 158, 256.

58 Solís José A. *Sayings, Proverbs, and Sentences: All the Treasure of the Popular Wisdom of the People of Spain at Your Fingertips.* Spain: El Arca de Papel Editores; 2003. p. 118.

59 *Dios Habla Hoy. The Bible with Deuterocanonical Books. Popular Version. Second Edition. Mexico City, D.F.: United Bible Societies; 1987. p. 127.*

60 *Feijóo S. The Knowledge of Juan Without Anything: Signs in the Expression of the People. Sayings. Santa Clara, Cuba. Signos Magazine. No. 14. Year 5, No. 2; January-April 1974. p. 149.*

61 *De la Luz y Caballero J. Aphorisms of José de la Luz y Caballero. Havana, Cuba: Biblioteca Popular de Clásicos Cubanos, Editorial Lex; 1960. p. 109.*

62 *Pérez Betancourt A, Moya Sánchez R, González Sánchez B. Error Hunting. Havana, Cuba: Editorial de Ciencias Sociales; 1990. p. 44.*

63 *Pérez Betancourt A, Moya Sánchez R, González Sánchez B. Error Hunting. Havana, Cuba: Editorial de Ciencias Sociales; 1990. p. 44.*

64 *Hesiod. In: Epictetus. Maxims, Exhortations, and Advice. Barcelona, Spain: Biblioteca Orientalista, Editorial Teosófica; 1922. p. 93.*

65 *Feijóo S. The Knowledge of Juan Without Anything: Signs in the Expression of the People. Sayings. Santa Clara, Cuba. Signos Magazine. No. 14. Year 5, No. 2; January-April 1974, p. 146.*

66 *Dios Habla Hoy. The Bible with Deuterocanonical Books. Popular Version. Second Edition. Mexico City, D.F.: United Bible Societies; 1987. p. 612.*

67 *Dios Habla Hoy. The Bible with Deuterocanonical Books. Popular Version. Second Edition. Mexico City, D.F.: United Bible Societies; 1987. p. 603.*

68 *Feijóo S. The Knowledge of Juan Without Anything: Signs in the Expression of the People. Sayings. Santa Clara, Cuba. Signos Magazine. No. 14. Year 5, No. 2; January-April 1974. p. 151.*

69 *Dios Habla Hoy. The Bible with Deuterocanonical Books. Popular Version. Second Edition. Mexico City, D.F.: United Bible Societies; 1987. p. 113.*

70 *We communicate not only through the meaning of our words but also through gestures, actions, mannerisms, body posture, tone of voice, and even our silence; with these, we might reveal what we should keep hidden.*

71 *Dios Habla Hoy. The Bible with Deuterocanonical Books. Popular Version. Second Edition. Mexico City, D.F.: United Bible Societies; 1987. p. 586.*

72 *Feijóo S. The Knowledge of Juan Without Anything: Signs in the Expression of the People. Sayings. Santa Clara, Cuba. Signos Magazine. No. 14. Year 5, No. 2; January-April 1974. p. 64.*

73 *Feijóo S. The Knowledge of Juan Without Anything: Signs in the Expression of the People. Sayings. Santa Clara, Cuba. Signos Magazine. No. 14. Year 5, No. 2; January-April 1974. p. 14.*

74 *Franklin B. Autobiography and Other Writings. No. 391. Mexico: Editorial Porrúa, S.A.; 1989. p. 112.*

75 *Feijóo S. From Compliments to Sayings: Oral Folklore of Cuba. Havana, Cuba: Editorial Letras Cubanas; 1981. p. 34.*

76 *Feijóo S. The Knowledge of Juan Without Anything: Signs in the Expression of the People. Sayings. Santa Clara, Cuba. Signos Magazine. No. 14. Year 5, No. 2; January-April 1974. p. 81.*

77 *Feijóo S. The Knowledge of Juan Without Anything: Signs in the Expression of the People. Sayings. Santa Clara, Cuba. Signos Magazine. No. 14. Year 5, No. 2; January-April 1974. p. 199.*

78 *Dios Habla Hoy. The Bible with Deuterocanonical Books. Popular Version. Second Edition. Mexico City, D.F.: United Bible Societies; 1987. p. 127.*

79 *Feijóo S. The Knowledge of Juan Without Anything: Signs in the Expression of the People. Sayings. Santa Clara, Cuba. Signos Magazine. No. 14. Year 5, No. 2; January-April 1974. p. 76.*

80 *Solís José A. Sayings, Proverbs, and Sentences: All the Treasure of the Popular Wisdom of the People of Spain at Your Fingertips. Spain: El Arca de Papel Editores; 2003. p. 58.*

81 *Solís José A. Sayings, Proverbs, and Sentences: All the Treasure of the Popular Wisdom of the People of Spain at Your Fingertips. Spain: El Arca de Papel Editores; 2003. p. 108.*

82 *United Bible Societies. Dios Habla Hoy: The Bible with Deuterocanonical Books. Popular Version. Second Edition. Old Testament. Proverbs. Mexico City, D.F.: United Bible Societies; 1987. p. 586.*

83 *Cannobbio Agustín. Chilean Sayings. Santiago de Chile: Encuadernación Barcelona; 1901. p. 89.*

84 *Dios Habla Hoy. The Bible with Deuterocanonical Books. Popular Version. Second Edition. Mexico City, D.F.: United Bible Societies; 1987. pp. 599, 605.*

85 *Dios Habla Hoy. The Bible with Deuterocanonical Books. Popular Version. Second Edition. Mexico City, D.F.: United Bible Societies; 1987. p. 607.*

86 *Feijóo S. From Compliments to Sayings: Oral Folklore of Cuba. Havana, Cuba: Editorial Letras Cubanas; 1981. p. 35.*

87 *Solís José A. Sayings, Proverbs, and Sentences: All the Treasure of the Popular Wisdom of the People of Spain at Your Fingertips. Spain: El Arca de Papel Editores; 2003. p. 127.*

88 *Feijóo S. From Compliments to Sayings: Oral Folklore of Cuba. Havana, Cuba: Editorial Letras Cubanas; 1981. p. 36.*

89 *The proverb collected by Samuel Feijóo is: "Never leave on the first try." In: Feijóo S. The Knowledge of Juan Without Anything: Signs in the Expression of the People. Sayings. Santa Clara, Cuba. Signos Magazine. No. 14. Year 5, No. 2; January-April 1974. p. 158.*

90 *Dios Habla Hoy. The Bible with Deuterocanonical Books. Popular Version. Second Edition. Mexico City, D.F.: United Bible Societies; 1987. p. 613.*

91 *Dios Habla Hoy. La Biblia con Deuterocanónicos. Versión Popular. Segunda Edición. México D.F. Sociedades Bíblicas Unidas; 1987. p.110.*

92 *Feijóo S. The Knowledge of Juan Without Anything: Signs in the Expression of the People. Sayings. Santa Clara, Cuba. Signos Magazine. No. 14. Year 5, No. 2; January-April 1974. p. 31.*

93 *Feijóo S. The Knowledge of Juan Without Anything: Signs in the Expression of the People. Sayings. Santa Clara, Cuba. Signos Magazine. No. 14. Year 5, No. 2; January-April 1974. p. 54.*

94 *Dios Habla Hoy. The Bible with Deuterocanonical Books. Popular Version. Second Edition. Mexico City, D.F.: United Bible Societies; 1987. p. 109.*

95 *Dios Habla Hoy. The Bible with Deuterocanonical Books. Popular Version. Second Edition. Mexico City, D.F.: United Bible Societies; 1987. p. 109.*

96 *Sintes Pros J. Dictionary of Aphorisms, Proverbs, and Sayings. Barcelona, Spain: Editorial Sintes; 1954. p. 290.*

97 *Maldonado Felipe CR. Being and Time: Themes of Spain, Classical Spanish Proverbs and Other Popular Sayings. Madrid, Spain: Taurus Ediciones S.A.; 1960. p. 44.*

98 Feijóo S. *The Knowledge of Juan Without Anything: Signs in the Expression of the People. Sayings.* Santa Clara, Cuba. Signos Magazine. No. 14. Year 5, No. 2; January-April 1974. p. 64.

99 Álvarez de los Ríos Tomás. *The Book of Proverbs.* Camagüey, Cuba: Editorial Ácana; 2017. p. 108.

100 Hall B. In: Sintes Pros J. *Great Dictionary of Famous Quotes.* Vol. II. Barcelona, Spain: Editorial Sintes; 1960. p. 395.

101 Solís José A. *Sayings, Proverbs, and Sentences: All the Treasure of the Popular Wisdom of the People of Spain at Your Fingertips.* Spain: El Arca de Papel Editores; 2003. p. 123.

102 Goethe: Quoted in: Sintes Pros, Jorge: *Great Dictionary of Famous Quotes.* Vol. II. Barcelona: Editorial Sintes, 1960. p. 395.

103 This idea appears in this version of the Tao Te King as follows: "He who conquers others is strong. He who conquers himself is the force." Lao Tsé. *Tao Te King. The Book of Tao.* XXXIII. Alejandría: Libros de Dominio Público. Available at: https://www.elejandria.com/libro/descargar/tao-te-king/tse-lao/107/137

104 Dios Habla Hoy. *The Bible with Deuterocanonical Books.* Popular Version. Second Edition. Mexico City, D.F.: United Bible Societies; 1987. p. 97.

105 Lao Tse. *Tao Teh Ching.* In: Lin Yutang. *Chinese Wisdom.* Buenos Aires, Argentina: Colección ACADEMUS, Biblioteca Nueva; 1945. p. 29.

106 Feijóo S. *The Knowledge of Juan Without Anything: Signs in the Expression of the People. Sayings.* Santa Clara, Cuba. Signos Magazine. No. 14. Year 5, No. 2; January-April 1974. p. 128.

107 Feijóo S. *The Knowledge of Juan Without Anything: Signs in the Expression of the People. Sayings.* Santa Clara, Cuba. Signos Magazine. No. 14. Year 5, No. 2; January-April 1974. p. 193.

108 Dios Habla Hoy. *The Bible with Deuterocanonical Books.* Popular Version. Second Edition. Mexico City, D.F.: United Bible Societies; 1987. p. 593.

109 Feijóo S. *The Knowledge of Juan Without Anything: Signs in the Expression of the People. Sayings.* Santa Clara, Cuba. Signos Magazine. No. 14. Year 5, No. 2; January-April 1974. p. 198.

110 Lao Tse. *Tao Te King.* Nueva Acrópolis. [Internet] Available at: http://www.nueva-acropolis.es

111 De Valbuena D. M. Complete Works of Marcus Tullius Cicero. Vol. IV. Madrid, Spain: Librería de la Viuda de Hernando y C; 1893. p. 114.

112 Feijóo, S. The Knowledge of Juan Without Anything: Signs in the Expression of the People. Sayings. Santa Clara, Cuba: Signos Journal, No. 14, Year 5, No. 2; January-April 1974, p. 57.

113 Seneca. In: Sintes Pros, J. Great Dictionary of Famous Quotes. Vol. II. Barcelona, Spain: Sintes Publishing; 1960, p. 396.

114 Dios Habla Hoy. The Bible with Deuterocanonicals. Popular Version. Second Edition. Mexico City, United Bible Societies; 1987, p. 127.

115 Feijóo, S. The Knowledge of Juan Without Anything: Signs in the Expression of the People. Sayings. Santa Clara, Cuba: Signos Journal, No. 14, Year 5, No. 2; January-April 1974, p. 114.

116 Feijóo, S. From Flattery to Sayings: Oral Folklore of Cuba. Havana, Cuba: Letras Cubanas Publishing; 1981, p. 38.

117 Feijóo, S. The Knowledge of Juan Without Anything: Signs in the Expression of the People. Sayings. Santa Clara, Cuba: Signos Journal, No. 14, Year 5, No. 2; January-April 1974, p. 194.

118 Dios Habla Hoy. The Bible with Deuterocanonicals. Popular Version. Second Edition. Mexico City, United Bible Societies; 1987, p. 607.

119 Dios Habla Hoy. The Bible with Deuterocanonicals. Popular Version. Second Edition. Mexico City, United Bible Societies; 1987, p. 94.

120 Franklin, B. Autobiography and Other Writings. No. 391. Mexico: Editorial Porrúa, S.A.; 1989, p. 113.

121 Dios Habla Hoy. The Bible with Deuterocanonicals. Popular Version. Second Edition. Mexico City, United Bible Societies; 1987, p. 97.

122 Feijóo, S. The Knowledge of Juan Without Anything: Signs in the Expression of the People. Sayings. Santa Clara, Cuba: Signos Journal, No. 14, Year 5, No. 2; January-April 1974, p. 133.

123 Dios Habla Hoy. The Bible with Deuterocanonicals. Popular Version. Second Edition. Mexico City, United Bible Societies; 1987, pp. 296-297.

124 Feijóo, S. The Knowledge of Juan Without Anything: Signs in the Expression of the People. Sayings. Santa Clara, Cuba: Signos Journal, No. 14, Year 5, No. 2; January-April 1974, p. 175.

125 Feijóo, S. The Knowledge of Juan Without Anything: Signs in the Expression of the People. Sayings. Santa Clara, Cuba: Signos Journal, No. 14, Year 5, No. 2; January-April 1974, p. 139.

126 Feijóo, S. The Knowledge of Juan Without Anything: Signs in the Expression of the People. Sayings. Santa Clara, Cuba: Signos Journal, No. 14, Year 5, No. 2; January-April 1974, p. 158.

127 Solís, José A. Proverbs, Sayings, and Sentences: All the Treasure of Popular Wisdom from the Peoples of Spain at Your Fingertips. Spain: El Arca de Papel Publishers; 2003, p. 79.

128 Feijóo, S. The Knowledge of Juan Without Anything: Signs in the Expression of the People. Sayings. Santa Clara, Cuba: Signos Journal, No. 14, Year 5, No. 2; January-April 1974, p. 32.

129 Feijóo, S. The Knowledge of Juan Without Anything: Signs in the Expression of the People. Sayings. Santa Clara, Cuba: Signos Journal, No. 14, Year 5, No. 2; January-April 1974, p. 78.

130 "...the human essence is not an abstraction inherent in each individual. In its reality, it is the ensemble of the social relations." (Marx, C. Theses on Feuerbach. In: Selected Works of Karl Marx and Frederick Engels. Vol. I. Moscow: Progress Publishers; 1973, p. 9)

131 Feijóo, S. From Flattery to Sayings: Oral Folklore of Cuba. Havana, Cuba: Letras Cubanas Publishing; 1981, p. 30.

132 Feijóo, S. The Knowledge of Juan Without Anything: Signs in the Expression of the People. Sayings. Santa Clara, Cuba: Signos Journal, No. 14, Year 5, No. 2; January-April 1974, p. 208.

133 Feijóo, S. The Knowledge of Juan Without Anything: Signs in the Expression of the People. Sayings. Santa Clara, Cuba: Signos Journal, No. 14, Year 5, No. 2; January-April 1974, p. 199.

134 Dios Habla Hoy. The Bible with Deuterocanonicals. Popular Version. Second Edition. Mexico City, United Bible Societies; 1987, p. 605.

135 Dios Habla Hoy. The Bible with Deuterocanonicals. Popular Version. Second Edition. Mexico City, United Bible Societies; 1987, p. 605.

136 Dios Habla Hoy. The Bible with Deuterocanonicals. Popular Version. Second Edition. Mexico City, United Bible Societies; 1987, p. 586.

137 Confucius. In: Lin Yutang. The Wisdom of Confucius. Buenos Aires, Argentina: Ediciones Siglo Veinte; 1952, p. 187.

138 Dios Habla Hoy. The Bible with Deuterocanonicals. Popular Version. Second Edition. Mexico City, United Bible Societies; 1987, p. 470.

139 Franklin, B. Autobiography and Other Writings. No. 391. Mexico: Editorial Porrúa, S.A.; 1989, p. 113.

140 Feijóo, S. The Wisdom of Juan Without Anything. Signs in the Expression of Peoples. Sayings. Santa Clara, Cuba: Revista Signos. No 14, Year 5, No 2; January-April 1974, p.199.

141 Epictetus. Maxims, Exhortations, and Advice. Barcelona, Spain: Biblioteca Orientalista, Editorial Teosófica; 1922, p.131.

142 Feijóo, S. The Wisdom of Juan Without Anything. Signs in the Expression of Peoples. Sayings. Santa Clara, Cuba: Revista Signos. No 14, Year 5, No 2; January-April 1974, p.199.

143 Feijóo, S. The Wisdom of Juan Without Anything. Signs in the Expression of Peoples. Sayings. Santa Clara, Cuba: Revista Signos. No 14, Year 5, No 2; January-April 1974, p.199.

144 "It is an adaptation of the biblical verse: I am sending you out like sheep among wolves. Therefore be as shrewd as snakes and as innocent as doves. (Matthew 10:16)"

145 Martí, J. The Strikes in the United States. North American Scenes. In: Complete Works, Vol. X. In the United States. Havana, Cuba: Editorial de Ciencias Sociales; 1991, p. 407.

146 Valdés Jane, E. Divinatory Sayings of the Snail and the Odun of Ifá. -In Cuban Santería- Documents for the History and Culture of Osha-Ifa in Cuba. Proverbs of (3-6) Ogundá tonti Obara. First Edition: Proyecto Orunmila; 2007, p. 10. https://www.academia.edu/8122356/Libro_de_Refranes_De_Diloggun_e_Ifa

147 Feijóo, S. The Wisdom of Juan Without Anything. Signs in the Expression of Peoples. Sayings. Santa Clara, Cuba: Revista Signos. No 14, Year 5, No 2; January-April 1974, p. 200.

148 Martí, J. Democratic Party Candidate for the Presidency of the United States. In: Complete Works, Vol. XIII. Havana, Cuba: Editorial de Ciencias Sociales; 1991, p. 278.

149 Confucius. In Lin Yutang. The Wisdom of Confucius. Buenos Aires, Argentina: Ediciones Siglo Veinte; 1952, p. 147.

150 Confucius. In: Lin Yutang. The Wisdom of Confucius. Buenos Aires, Argentina: Ediciones Siglo Veinte; 1952, p. 29.

151 Dios Habla Hoy. The Bible with Deuterocanonicals. Popular Version. Second Edition. Mexico City, Mexico: United Bible Societies; 1987, pp. 7, 71.

152 Vishnu Sarma. Panchatantra. Havana, Cuba: Editorial Arte y Literatura; 1989, p. 298.

153 Feijóo, S. The Wisdom of Juan Without Anything. Signs in the Expression of Peoples. Sayings. Santa Clara, Cuba: Revista Signos. No 14, Year 5, No 2; January-April 1974, p. 191.

154 Sintes Pros, J. Dictionary of Aphorisms, Proverbs, and Sayings. Barcelona, Spain: Editorial Sintes; 1954, p. 224.

155 Da Vinci, L. In: Sintes Pros, J. Great Dictionary of Famous Quotes. Vol. I. Barcelona, Spain: Editorial Sintes; 1960, p. 206.

156 Something similar happens when the immune system is depressed, and the body is attacked by trivial germs with which it coexisted without problems when the defensive system functioned optimally.

157 Feijóo, S. The Wisdom of Juan Without Anything. Signs in the Expression of Peoples. Sayings. Santa Clara, Cuba: Revista Signos. No 14, Year 5, No 2; January-April 1974, p. 81.

158 Feijóo, S. The Wisdom of Juan Without Anything. Signs in the Expression of Peoples. Sayings. Santa Clara, Cuba: Revista Signos. No 14, Year 5, No 2; January-April 1974, p. 68.

159 Feijóo, S. The Wisdom of Juan Without Anything. Signs in the Expression of Peoples. Sayings. Santa Clara, Cuba: Revista Signos. No 14, Year 5, No 2; January-April 1974, p. 151.

160 Feijóo, S. From Compliment to Witty Remark, Oral Folklore of Cuba. Havana, Cuba: Editorial Letras Cubanas; 1981, p. 44.

161 Feijóo, S. The Wisdom of Juan Without Anything. Signs in the Expression of Peoples. Sayings. Santa Clara, Cuba: Revista Signos. No 14, Year 5, No 2; January-April 1974, p. 77.

162 Feijóo, S. The Wisdom of Juan Without Anything. Signs in the Expression of Peoples. Sayings. Santa Clara, Cuba: Revista Signos. No 14, Year 5, No 2; January-April 1974, p. 77.

163 Feijóo, S. The Wisdom of Juan Without Anything. Signs in the Expression of Peoples. Sayings. Santa Clara, Cuba: Revista Signos. No 14, Year 5, No 2; January-April 1974, p. 194.

164 Feijóo, S. The Wisdom of Juan Without Anything. Signs in the Expression of Peoples. Sayings. Santa Clara, Cuba: Revista Signos. No 14, Year 5, No 2; January-April 1974, p. 186.

165 Feijóo, S. The Wisdom of Juan Without Anything. Signs in the Expression of Peoples. Sayings. Santa Clara, Cuba: Revista Signos. No 14, Year 5, No 2; January-April 1974, p. 143.

166 *Feijóo, S. The Wisdom of Juan Without Anything. Signs in the Expression of Peoples. Sayings. Santa Clara, Cuba: Revista Signos. No 14, Year 5, No 2; January-April 1974, p. 195.*

167 *Sintes Pros, J. Dictionary of Aphorisms, Proverbs, and Sayings. Barcelona, Spain: Editorial Sintes; 1954, p. 247.*

168 *Feijóo, S. The Wisdom of Juan Without Anything. Signs in the Expression of Peoples. Sayings. Santa Clara, Cuba: Revista Signos. No 14, Year 5, No 2; January-April 1974, p. 85.*

169 *In this way, what initially were merely assumptions based on incorrect interpretations of others' actions and gestures becomes a reality.*

170 *Sintes Pros, J. Dictionary of Aphorisms, Proverbs, and Sayings. Barcelona, Spain: Editorial Sintes; 1954, p. 255.*

171 *Quevedo y Villegas, F. In: The Author and His Work. Havana, Cuba: Instituto Cubano del Libro, Editorial Pueblo y Educación; 1974, p. 32.*

172 *Sintes Pros, J. Dictionary of Aphorisms, Proverbs, and Sayings. Barcelona, Spain: Editorial Sintes; 1954, p. 254.*

173 *Sintes Pros, J. Dictionary of Aphorisms, Proverbs, and Sayings. Barcelona, Spain: Editorial Sintes; 1954, p. 313.*

174 *Dios Habla Hoy. The Bible with Deuterocanonicals. Popular Version. Second Edition. Mexico City, Mexico: United Bible Societies; 1987, p. 94.*

175 *Franklyn, B. In: Clavel, Vicente. When Great Inventors Were Children. Havana, Cuba: Editorial Gente Nueva; 1978, p. 12.*

176 *Martí, J. In the United States of America. Letters, Painting, and Various Articles. In: Complete Works, Vol. XIII. Havana, Cuba: Editorial de Ciencias Sociales; 1991, p. 278.*

177 *Dios Habla Hoy. The Bible with Deuterocanonicals. Popular Version. Second Edition. Mexico City, Mexico: United Bible Societies; 1987, p. 253.*

178 *Valdés Jane, E. Divinatory Sayings of the Snail and the Odun of Ifá. -In Cuban Santería- Documents for the History and Culture of Osha-Ifa in Cuba. First Edition: Proyecto Orunmila; 2007, p. 16. Available at URL: https://www.academia.edu/8122356/Libro_de_Refranes_De_Diloggun_e_Ifa*

179 *Solís José, A. Proverbs, Sayings, and Sentences. All the Treasure of Popular Wisdom from the Peoples of Spain at Your Fingertips. Spain: El Arca de Papel Editores; 2003, p. 115.*

180 *Unlike anxiety, with fear, the individual can pinpoint the specific object or circumstance that causes it.*

181 On occasion, under the influence of fear, extraordinary actions are performed, which the individual finds very difficult to repeat once the emergency feels over.

182 Sintes Pros, J. Dictionary of Aphorisms, Proverbs, and Sayings. Barcelona, Spain: Editorial Sintes; 1954, p. 137.

183 Sintes Pros, J. Dictionary of Aphorisms, Proverbs, and Sayings. Barcelona, Spain: Editorial Sintes; 1954, p. 285.

184 Feijóo, S. The Wisdom of Juan Without Anything. Signs in the Expression of Peoples. Sayings. Santa Clara, Cuba: Revista Signos. No 14, Year 5, No 2; January-April 1974, p. 201.

185 Feijóo, S. From Compliment to Witty Remark, Oral Folklore of Cuba. Havana, Cuba: Editorial Letras Cubanas; 1981, p. 25.

186 Feijóo, S. The Wisdom of Juan Without Anything. Signs in the Expression of Peoples. Sayings. Santa Clara, Cuba: Revista Signos. No 14, Year 5, No 2; January-April 1974, p. 110.

187 Feijóo, S. The Wisdom of Juan Without Anything. Signs in the Expression of Peoples. Sayings. Santa Clara, Cuba: Revista Signos. No 14, Year 5, No 2; January-April 1974, p. 150.

188 Feijóo, S. The Wisdom of Juan Without Anything. Signs in the Expression of Peoples. Sayings. Santa Clara, Cuba: Revista Signos. No 14, Year 5, No 2; January-April 1974, p. 112.

189 Dios Habla Hoy. The Bible with Deuterocanonicals. Popular Version. Second Edition. Mexico City, Mexico: United Bible Societies; 1987, p. 95.

190 Feijóo, S. The Wisdom of Juan Without Anything. Signs in the Expression of Peoples. Sayings. Santa Clara, Cuba: Revista Signos. No 14, Year 5, No 2; January-April 1974, p. 110.

191 Feijóo, S. The Wisdom of Juan Without Anything. Signs in the Expression of Peoples. Sayings. Santa Clara, Cuba: Revista Signos. No 14, Year 5, No 2; January-April 1974, p. 156.

192 Solís José, A. Proverbs, Sayings, and Sentences. All the Treasure of Popular Wisdom from the Peoples of Spain at Your Fingertips. Spain: El Arca de Papel Editores; 2003, p. 57.

193 Feijóo, S. The Wisdom of Juan Without Anything. Signs in the Expression of Peoples. Sayings. Santa Clara, Cuba: Revista Signos. No 14, Year 5, No 2; January-April 1974, p. 173.

194 Valdés Jane, E. Divinatory Sayings of the Snail and the Odun of Ifá. -In Cuban Santería- Documents for the History and Culture of Osha-Ifa in

Cuba. Proverbs of (4-13) Iroso tonti Metanlá. First Edition: Proyecto Orunmila; 2007, p. 16. Available at URL: https://www.academia.edu/8122356/Libro_de_Refranes_De_Diloggun_e_Ifa

195 Feijóo, S. The Wisdom of Juan Without Anything. Signs in the Expression of Peoples. Sayings. Santa Clara, Cuba: Revista Signos. No 14, Year 5, No 2; January-April 1974, p. 137.

196 Feijóo, S. The Wisdom of Juan Without Anything. Signs in the Expression of Peoples. Sayings. Santa Clara, Cuba: Revista Signos. No 14, Year 5, No 2; January-April 1974, p. 158.

197 Sintes Pros, J. Dictionary of Aphorisms, Proverbs, and Sayings. Barcelona, Spain: Editorial Sintes; 1954, p. 254.

198 Feijóo, S. From Compliment to Witty Remark, Oral Folklore of Cuba. Havana, Cuba: Editorial Letras Cubanas; 1981, p. 32.

199 Feijóo, S. From Compliment to Witty Remark, Oral Folklore of Cuba. Havana, Cuba: Editorial Letras Cubanas; 1981, p. 26.

200 Dios Habla Hoy. The Bible with Deuterocanonicals. Popular Version. Second Edition. Mexico City, Mexico: United Bible Societies; 1987, p. 94.

201 Feijóo, S. The Wisdom of Juan Without Anything. Signs in the Expression of Peoples. Sayings. Santa Clara, Cuba: Revista Signos. No 14, Year 5, No 2; January-April 1974, p. 143.

202 Dios Habla Hoy. The Bible with Deuterocanonicals. Popular Version. Second Edition. Mexico City, Mexico: United Bible Societies; 1987, p. 591.

203 Dios Habla Hoy. The Bible with Deuterocanonicals. Popular Version. Second Edition. Mexico City, Mexico: United Bible Societies; 1987, p. 95.

204 Feijóo, S. The Wisdom of Juan Without Anything. Signs in the Expression of Peoples. Sayings. Santa Clara, Cuba: Revista Signos. No 14, Year 5, No 2; January-April 1974, p. 52.

205 Dios Habla Hoy. The Bible with Deuterocanonicals. Popular Version. Second Edition. Mexico City, Mexico: United Bible Societies; 1987, p. 124.

206 Sintes Pros, J. Dictionary of Aphorisms, Proverbs, and Sayings. Barcelona, Spain: Editorial Sintes; 1954, p. 50.

207 Feijóo, S. The Wisdom of Juan Without Anything. Signs in the Expression of Peoples. Sayings. Santa Clara, Cuba: Revista Signos. No 14, Year 5, No 2; January-April 1974, p. 158.

208 Sintes Pros, J. Dictionary of Aphorisms, Proverbs, and Sayings. Barcelona, Spain: Editorial Sintes; 1954, p. 85.

209 Feijóo, S. *The Wisdom of Juan Without Anything. Signs in the Expression of Peoples. Sayings.* Santa Clara, Cuba: Revista Signos. No 14, Year 5, No 2; January-April 1974, p. 195.

210 Feijóo, S. *The Wisdom of Juan Without Anything. Signs in the Expression of Peoples. Sayings.* Santa Clara, Cuba: Revista Signos. No 14, Year 5, No 2; January-April 1974, p. 67.

211 Feijóo, S. *The Wisdom of Juan Without Anything. Signs in the Expression of Peoples. Sayings.* Santa Clara, Cuba: Revista Signos. No 14, Year 5, No 2; January-April 1974, p. 191.

212 Feijóo, S. *The Wisdom of Juan Without Anything. Signs in the Expression of Peoples. Sayings.* Santa Clara, Cuba: Revista Signos. No 14, Year 5, No 2; January-April 1974, p. 152.

213 Feijóo, S. *The Wisdom of Juan Without Anything. Signs in the Expression of Peoples. Sayings.* Santa Clara, Cuba: Revista Signos. No 14, Year 5, No 2; January-April 1974, p. 29.

214 Álvarez de los Ríos, Tomás. *The Book of Sayings.* Camagüey, Cuba: Editorial Ácana; 2017, p. 31.

215 Feijóo, S. *The Wisdom of Juan Without Anything. Signs in the Expression of Peoples. Saying.* Santa Clara, Cuba: Revista Signos. No 14, Year 5, No 2; January-April 1974, p. 198.

216 *The amount of time and effort is essential to achieving excellence in any activity, but so is the quality of this dedicated time, along with motivation and access to adequate resources.*

217 Feijóo, S. *The Wisdom of Juan Without Anything. Signs in the Expression of Peoples. Saying.* Santa Clara, Cuba: Revista Signos. No 14, Year 5, No 2; January-April 1974, p. 198.

218 Feijóo, S. *The Wisdom of Juan Without Anything. Signs in the Expression of Peoples. Saying.* Santa Clara, Cuba: Revista Signos. No 14, Year 5, No 2; January-April 1974, p. 203.

219 Martí, J. *Letter to José Dolores Poyo, New York, July 7, 1894. In: Complete Works, Vol. III.* Havana, Cuba: Editorial de Ciencias Sociales; 1991, p. 225.

220 Feijóo, S. *The Wisdom of Juan Without Anything. Signs in the Expression of Peoples. Saying.* Santa Clara, Cuba: Revista Signos. No 14, Year 5, No 2; January-April 1974, p. 186.

221 *Dios Habla Hoy. The Bible with Deuterocanonicals. Popular Version. Second Edition.* Mexico City, Mexico: United Bible Societies; 1987, p. 612.

222 Feijóo, S. *The Wisdom of Juan Without Anything. Signs in the Expression of Peoples. Saying.* Santa Clara, Cuba: Revista Signos. No 14, Year 5, No 2; January-April 1974, p. 163.

223 *Some call luck the coincidence of opportunity with the ability to seize it.*

224 Feijóo, S. *The Wisdom of Juan Without Anything. Signs in the Expression of Peoples. Saying.* Santa Clara, Cuba: Revista Signos. No 14, Year 5, No 2; January-April 1974, p. 189.

225 Feijóo, S. *The Wisdom of Juan Without Anything. Signs in the Expression of Peoples. Saying.* Santa Clara, Cuba: Revista Signos. No 14, Year 5, No 2; January-April 1974, p. 200.

226 Feijóo, S. *The Wisdom of Juan Without Anything. Signs in the Expression of Peoples. Saying.* Santa Clara, Cuba: Revista Signos. No 14, Year 5, No 2; January-April 1974, p. 151.

227 *Dios Habla Hoy. The Bible with Deuterocanonicals. Popular Version. Second Edition.* Mexico City, Mexico: United Bible Societies; 1987, p. 595.

228 Sintes Pros, J. *Dictionary of Aphorisms, Proverbs, and Sayings.* Barcelona, Spain: Editorial Sintes; 1954, p. 231.

229 Feijóo, S. *The Wisdom of Juan Without Anything. Signs in the Expression of Peoples. Saying.* Santa Clara, Cuba: Revista Signos. No 14, Year 5, No 2; January-April 1974, p. 59.

230 Feijóo, S. *The Wisdom of Juan Without Anything. Signs in the Expression of Peoples. Saying.* Santa Clara, Cuba: Revista Signos. No 14, Year 5, No 2; January-April 1974, p. 159.

231 Feijóo, S. *The Wisdom of Juan Without Anything. Signs in the Expression of Peoples. Saying.* Santa Clara, Cuba: Revista Signos. No 14, Year 5, No 2; January-April 1974, p. 158.

232 Feijóo, S. *The Wisdom of Juan Without Anything. Signs in the Expression of Peoples. Saying.* Santa Clara, Cuba: Revista Signos. No 14, Year 5, No 2; January-April 1974, p. 32.

233 Valdés Jane, E. *Divinatory Sayings of the Snail and the Odun of Ifá. -In Cuban Santería- Documents for the History and Culture of Osha-Ifa in Cuba. Proverbs of (8-5) Eyeúnle tonti Oshé and Ogbe She.* First Edition: Proyecto Orunmila; 2007, pp. 31 and 74. https://www.academia.edu/8122356/Libro_de_Refranes_De_Diloggun_e_Ifa

234 Flores-Huerta, S. *Sayings or Proverbs. Thematic Compendium.* Mexico: CopIt-arXives; 2016, p. 30. Available at: http://scifunam.fisica.unam.mx/mir/copit/CD0006ES/CD0006ES.pdf

235 *Lao Tzu. Tao Teh Ching. In: Lin Yutang. Chinese Wisdom. Buenos Aires, Argentina: Colección ACADEMUS, Biblioteca Nueva; 1945, p. 39.*

236 *Valdés Jane, E. Divinatory Sayings of the Snail and the Odun of Ifá. -In Cuban Santería- Documents for the History and Culture of Osha-Ifa in Cuba. Sayings of (1-11) Okana tonti Ojuani. First Edition: Proyecto Orunmila; 2007, p. 4. Available at URL: https://www.academia.edu/8122356/Libro_de_Refranes_De_Diloggun_e_Ifa*

237 *Feijóo, S. The Wisdom of Juan Without Anything. Signs in the Expression of Peoples. Saying. Santa Clara, Cuba: Revista Signos. No 14, Year 5, No 2; January-April 1974, p. 32.*

238 *Feijóo, S. The Wisdom of Juan Without Anything. Signs in the Expression of Peoples. Saying. Santa Clara, Cuba: Revista Signos. No 14, Year 5, No 2; January-April 1974, p. 143.*

239 *Feijóo, S. The Knowledge and Song of Juan Without Anything. Havana, Cuba: Editorial Letras Cubanas; 1984, p. 197.*

240 *Saadi. In: Feijóo, S. The Wisdom of Juan Without Anything. Signs in the Expression of Peoples. Saying. Santa Clara, Cuba: Revista Signos. No 14, Year 5, No 2; January-April 1974, p. 24.*

241 *Solís José, A. Sayings, Proverbs, and Sentences. All the Treasure of Popular Wisdom from the Peoples of Spain at Your Fingertips. Spain: El Arca de Papel Editores; 2003, p. 134.*

242 *Valdés Jane, E. Divinatory Sayings of the Snail and the Odun of Ifá. -In Cuban Santería- Documents for the History and Culture of Osha-Ifa in Cuba. Sayings of (4-8) Iroso tonti Eyeúnle, (8-7) Eyeúnle tonti Odí, Ika Ogunda, and Oshe Meyi. First Edition: Proyecto Orunmila; 2007, pp. 15, 32, 109, and 120. Available at URL: https://www.academia.edu/8122356/Libro_de_Refranes_De_Diloggun_e_Ifa*

243 *Confucius. In: Lin Yutang. Chinese Wisdom. Buenos Aires, Argentina: Colección ACADEMUS, Biblioteca Nueva; 1945, p. 291.*

244 *Solís José, A. Sayings, Proverbs, and Sentences. All the Treasure of Popular Wisdom from the Peoples of Spain at Your Fingertips. Spain: El Arca de Papel Editores; 2003, p. 127.*

245 *Solís José, A. Sayings, Proverbs, and Sentences. All the Treasure of Popular Wisdom from the Peoples of Spain at Your Fingertips. Spain: El Arca de Papel Editores; 2003, p. 89.*

246 *Solís José, A. Sayings, Proverbs, and Sentences. All the Treasure of Popular Wisdom from the Peoples of Spain at Your Fingertips. Spain: El Arca de Papel Editores; 2003, p. 109.*

247 *Solís José, A. Sayings, Proverbs, and Sentences. All the Treasure of Popular Wisdom from the Peoples of Spain at Your Fingertips. Spain: El Arca de Papel Editores; 2003, p. 41.*

248 *Feijóo, S. The Wisdom of Juan Without Anything. Signs in the Expression of Peoples. Saying. Santa Clara, Cuba: Revista Signos. No 14, Year 5, No 2; January-April 1974, p. 59.*

249 *Solís José, A. Sayings, Proverbs, and Sentences. All the Treasure of Popular Wisdom from the Peoples of Spain at Your Fingertips. Spain: El Arca de Papel Editores; 2003, p. 154.*

250 *Feijóo, S. The Wisdom of Juan Without Anything. Signs in the Expression of Peoples. Saying. Santa Clara, Cuba: Revista Signos. No 14, Year 5, No 2; January-April 1974, p. 63.*

251 *Solís José, A. Sayings, Proverbs, and Sentences. All the Treasure of Popular Wisdom from the Peoples of Spain at Your Fingertips. Spain: El Arca de Papel Editores; 2003, p. 30.*

252 *Solís José, A. Sayings, Proverbs, and Sentences. All the Treasure of Popular Wisdom from the Peoples of Spain at Your Fingertips. Spain: El Arca de Papel Editores; 2003, p. 71.*

253 *Solís José, A. Sayings, Proverbs, and Sentences. All the Treasure of Popular Wisdom from the Peoples of Spain at Your Fingertips. Spain: El Arca de Papel Editores; 2003, p. 153.*

254 *Feijóo, S. The Wisdom of Juan Without Anything. Signs in the Expression of Peoples. Saying. Santa Clara, Cuba: Revista Signos. No 14, Year 5, No 2; January-April 1974, p. 187.*

255 *Dios Habla Hoy. The Bible with Deuterocanonicals. Popular Version. Second Edition. Mexico City, Mexico: United Bible Societies; 1987, p. 594.*

256 *Feijóo, S. The Wisdom of Juan Without Anything. Signs in the Expression of Peoples. Saying. Santa Clara, Cuba: Revista Signos. No 14, Year 5, No 2; January-April 1974, p. 139.*

257 *Símonov P. Motivation of the Brain. Moscow: Mir Publishers; 1987. p. 65.*

258 *Sintes Pros J. Dictionary of Aphorisms, Proverbs, and Sayings. Barcelona, Spain: Editorial Sintes; 1954. p. 88.*

259 Feijóo S. *The Wisdom of Juan Without Anything. Signs in the Expression of Peoples. Saying*. Santa Clara, Cuba: Revista Signos. No 14, Year 5, No 2; January-April 1974. p. 99.

260 Solís José A. *Proverbs, Sayings, and Sentences: The Complete Treasure of Popular Wisdom from the People of Spain at Your Fingertips*. Spain: El Arca de Papel Editores; 2003. p. 95.

261 Feijóo S. *The Wisdom of Juan Without Anything. Signs in the Expression of Peoples. Saying*. Santa Clara, Cuba: Revista Signos. No 14, Year 5, No 2; January-April 1974. p. 210.

262 Solís José A. *Proverbs, Sayings, and Sentences: The Complete Treasure of Popular Wisdom from the People of Spain at Your Fingertips*. Spain: El Arca de Papel Editores; 2003. p. 59.

263 Valdés Jane E. *Divinatory Sayings of the Caracol and the Odun of Ifá in Cuban Santería: Documents for the History and Culture of Osha-Ifá in Cuba. Sayings of (5-15) Oshé tonti Marunlá*. 1st ed. Proyecto Orunmila; 2007. p. 20. Available at: https://www.academia.edu/8122356/Libro_de_Refranes_De_Diloggun_e_Ifa

264 Feijóo S. *The Wisdom of Juan Without Anything. Signs in the Expression of Peoples. Saying*. Santa Clara, Cuba: Revista Signos. No 14, Year 5, No 2; January-April 1974. p. 100.

265 Álvarez de los Ríos T. *The Book of Sayings*. Camagüey, Cuba: Editorial Ácana; 2017. p. 103.

266 One Hundred Proverbs by Mr. Tut-Tut. In: Lin Yutang. *Chinese Wisdom*. Buenos Aires, Argentina: ACADEMUS Collection, Biblioteca Nueva; 1945. p. 671.

267 Feijóo S. *The Wisdom of Juan Without Anything. Signs in the Expression of Peoples. Saying*. Santa Clara, Cuba: Revista Signos. No 14, Year 5, No 2; January-April 1974. p. 163.

268 Vishnu Sarma. Panchatantra. In: Feijóo S. *The Wisdom of Juan Without Anything. Signs in the Expression of Peoples. Saying*. Santa Clara, Cuba: Revista Signos. No 14, Year 5, No 2; January-April 1974. p. 15.

269 Valdés Jane E. *Divinatory Sayings of the Caracol and the Odun of Ifá in Cuban Santería: Documents for the History and Culture of Osha-Ifá in Cuba. Sayings of (1-6) Okana tonti Obara*. 1st ed. Proyecto Orunmila; 2007. p. 2. Available at: https://www.academia.edu/8122356/Libro_de_Refranes_De_Diloggun_e_Ifa

270 Feijóo S. *The Wisdom of Juan Without Anything. Signs in the Expression of Peoples. Saying. Santa Clara, Cuba: Revista Signos. No 14, Year 5, No 2; January-April 1974. p. 158.*

271 Feijóo S. *The Wisdom of Juan Without Anything. Signs in the Expression of Peoples. Saying. Santa Clara, Cuba: Revista Signos. No 14, Year 5, No 2; January-April 1974. p. 24.*

272 *El refrán que aparece en la recopilación de Samuel Feijóo es: "Es un árbol malo el que cae al primer hachazo." (Feijóo S. The Wisdom of Juan Without Anything. Signs in the Expression of Peoples. Saying. Santa Clara, Cuba: Revista Signos. No 14, Year 5, No 2; January-April 1974. p. 146).*

273 Dios Habla Hoy. *The Bible with Deuterocanonical Books: Popular Version. 2nd ed. Mexico City: Sociedades Bíblicas Unidas; 1987. p. 601.*

274 *Franklyn B. Autobiography and Other Writings. No 391. Mexico: Editorial Porrúa, S.A.; 1989. p. 113.*

275 Confucius. *In: Lin Yutang. Chinese Wisdom. Buenos Aires, Argentina: ACADEMUS Collection, Biblioteca Nueva; 1945. p. 312.*

276 Feijóo S. *The Wisdom of Juan Without Anything. Signs in the Expression of Peoples. Saying. Santa Clara, Cuba: Revista Signos. No 14, Year 5, No 2; January-April 1974. p. 156.*

277 Feijóo S. *The Wisdom of Juan Without Anything. Signs in the Expression of Peoples. Saying. Santa Clara, Cuba: Revista Signos. No 14, Year 5, No 2; January-April 1974. p. 153.*

278 Chinese Aphorisms. *In: Lin Yutang. Chinese Wisdom. Buenos Aires, Argentina: ACADEMUS Collection, Biblioteca Nueva; 1945. p. 595.*

279 ao Tzu. *Tao Teh Ching. In: Lin Yutang. Chinese Wisdom. Buenos Aires, Argentina: ACADEMUS Collection, Biblioteca Nueva; 1945. p. 59.*

280 Feijóo S. *The Wisdom of Juan Without Anything. Signs in the Expression of Peoples. Saying. Santa Clara, Cuba: Revista Signos. No 14, Year 5, No 2; January-April 1974. p. 53.*

281 Solís José A. *Sayings, Proverbs, Expressions, and Sentences: The Complete Treasure of Popular Wisdom from the People of Spain at Your Fingertips. Spain: El Arca de Papel Editores; 2003. p. 111.*

282 Dios Habla Hoy. *The Bible with Deuterocanonical Books: Popular Version. 2nd ed. Mexico City: Sociedades Bíblicas Unidas; 1987. p. 103.*

283 Chuang Tzu. *The Equalization of All Things. In: Lin Yutang. Chinese Wisdom. Buenos Aires, Argentina: ACADEMUS Collection, Biblioteca Nueva; 1945. p. 79.*

284 Chuang Tzu. Autumn Floods. In: Lin Yutang. Chinese Wisdom. Buenos Aires, Argentina: ACADEMUS Collection, Biblioteca Nueva; 1945. p. 137.

285 Solís José A. Sayings, Proverbs, Expressions, and Sentences: The Complete Treasure of Popular Wisdom from the People of Spain at Your Fingertips. Spain: El Arca de Papel Editores; 2003. p. 97.

286 Feijóo S. From Compliments to Sayings: Oral Folklore of Cuba. Havana, Cuba: Editorial Letras Cubanas; 1981. p. 26.

287 Confucius. In: Lin Yutang. The Wisdom of Confucius. Buenos Aires, Argentina: Ediciones Siglo Veinte; 1952. p. 142.

288 Confucius. In: Lin Yutang. Chinese Wisdom. Buenos Aires, Argentina: ACADEMUS Collection, Biblioteca Nueva; 1945. p. 327.

289 Confucius. In: Lin Yutang. Chinese Wisdom. Buenos Aires, Argentina: ACADEMUS Collection, Biblioteca Nueva; 1945. p. 310.

290 Dios Habla Hoy. The Bible with Deuterocanonical Books: Popular Version. 2nd ed. Mexico City: Sociedades Bíblicas Unidas; 1987. p. 590.

291 Dios Habla Hoy. The Bible with Deuterocanonical Books: Popular Version. 2nd ed. Mexico City: Sociedades Bíblicas Unidas; 1987. p. 604.

292 Feijóo S. The Wisdom of Juan Without Anything. Signs in the Expression of Peoples. Saying. Santa Clara, Cuba: Revista Signos. No 14, Year 5, No 2; January-April 1974. p. 137.

293 Seneca. In: Sintes Pros J. Great Dictionary of Famous Quotes. Barcelona, Spain: Editorial Sintes. Vol. III; 1960. p. 267.

294 Feijóo S. From Compliments to Sayings: Oral Folklore of Cuba. Havana, Cuba: Editorial Letras Cubanas; 1981. p. 28.

295 It's interesting to see how people who have experienced the same loss and have similar reasons to suffer can recover at different rates. Sometimes, even the person who takes the longest to recover is not the one with the most justifications for being distressed. Occasionally, an individual may remain in a state of grief because they have secondary gains: it suits them to stay sad in order to continue avoiding the responsibilities that their state of affliction has provided.

296 Feijóo S. The Wisdom of Juan Without Anything. Signs in the Expression of Peoples. Saying. Santa Clara, Cuba: Revista Signos. No 14, Year 5, No 2; January-April 1974. p. 195.

297 Flores-Huerta S. Sayings or Proverbs: Thematic Compendium. Mexico: CopIt-arXives; 2016. p. 32. Available at: http://scifunam.fisica.unam.mx/mir/copit/CD0006ES/CD0006ES.pdf

298 Sintes Pros J. *Dictionary of Aphorisms, Proverbs, and Sayings.* Barcelona, Spain: Editorial Sintes; 1954. p. 234.

299 Feijóo S. *The Wisdom of Juan Without Anything. Signs in the Expression of Peoples. Saying.* Santa Clara, Cuba: Revista Signos. No 14, Year 5, No 2; January-April 1974. p. 127.

300 Sintes Pros J. *Dictionary of Aphorisms, Proverbs, and Sayings.* Barcelona, Spain: Editorial Sintes; 1954. p. 292.

301 Martí J. *Complete Works. Vol. II. Commemorative Edition for the Fiftieth Anniversary of His Death.* Havana, Cuba: Editorial Lex; 1946. p. 1848.

302 Sintes Pros J. *Dictionary of Aphorisms, Proverbs, and Sayings.* Barcelona, Spain: Editorial Sintes; 1954. p. 291.

303 Martí J. *Complete Works. Vol. II. Commemorative Edition for the Fiftieth Anniversary of His Death.* Havana, Cuba: Editorial Lex; 1946. p. 1669.

304 Flores-Huerta S. *Sayings or Proverbs: Thematic Compendium.* Mexico: CopIt-arXives; 2016. p. 29. Available at: http://scifunam.fisica.unam.mx/mir/copit/CD0006ES/CD0006ES.pdf

305 Feijóo S. *The Wisdom of Juan Without Anything: Signs in the Expression of the Peoples. Saying.* Santa Clara, Cuba: Revista Signos. No 14, Year 5, No 2; January-April 1974. p. 57.

306 Feijóo S. *The Wisdom of Juan Without Anything: Signs in the Expression of the Peoples. Saying.* Santa Clara, Cuba: Revista Signos. No 14, Year 5, No 2; January-April 1974. p. 172.

307 Feijóo S. *The Wisdom of Juan Without Anything: Signs in the Expression of the Peoples. Saying.* Santa Clara, Cuba: Revista Signos. No 14, Year 5, No 2; January-April 1974. p. 52.

308 Feijóo S. *The Wisdom of Juan Without Anything: Signs in the Expression of the Peoples. Saying.* Santa Clara, Cuba: Revista Signos. No 14, Year 5, No 2; January-April 1974. p. 86.

309 Feijóo S. *From the Compliment to the Remark: Oral Folklore of Cuba.* Havana, Cuba: Editorial Letras Cubanas; 1981. p. 59.

310 Valdés Jane E. *Divinatory Sayings of the Snail and the Odun of Ifá: In Cuban Santería: Documents for the History and Culture of Osha-Ifá in Cuba. Sayings from (6-15) Obara tonti Marunlá.* First Edition: Proyecto Orunmila; 2007. p. 24. Available at: https://www.academia.edu/8122356/Libro_de_Refranes_De_Diloggun_e_Ifa

311 Valdés Jane E. Divinatory Sayings of the Snail and the Odun of Ifá: In Cuban Santería: Documents for the History and Culture of Osha-Ifá in Cuba. Sayings from (8-9) Eyeúnle tonti Osá. First Edition: Proyecto Orunmila; 2007. p. 33. Available at: https://www.academia.edu/8122356/Libro_de_Refranes_De_Diloggun_e_Ifa

312 Valdés Jane E. Divinatory Sayings of the Snail and the Odun of Ifá: In Cuban Santería: Documents for the History and Culture of Osha-Ifá in Cuba. Sayings from (9-5) Osá tonti Oshé. First Edition: Proyecto Orunmila; 2007. p. 36. Available at: https://www.academia.edu/8122356/Libro_de_Refranes_De_Diloggun_e_Ifa

313 Lao Tzu: Tao Te Ching, Casa del Escritor Habanero, Havana, 1991, p. 27.

314 Solís José A. Sayings, Proverbs, and Maxims: The Entire Treasure of Popular Wisdom from the Peoples of Spain at Your Reach. Spain. El Arca de Papel Editores; 2003. p. 115.

315 Erasmus D. Complete Works. Madrid, Spain. Editorial Aguilar; 1956. p. 571.

316 Lao Tzu. Tao Te Ching. Havana, Cuba. Cuadernos La Puerta de Papel. Provincial Center of Books and Literature; 1991. p. 28.

317 Martí, J. Complete Works. Vol. II. Commemorative Edition of the Fiftieth Anniversary of His Death. Havana, Cuba. Editorial Lex; 1946. p. 1846.

318 Feijóo, S. The Knowledge of Juan with Nothing. Signs in the Expression of the Peoples. Saying. Santa Clara, Cuba: Signos Magazine. No. 14. Year 5, No. 2; January-April 1974. p. 105.

319 Lao Tzu. Tao Teh Ching. In: Lin Yutang. Chinese Wisdom. Buenos Aires, Argentina: ACADEMUS Collection, Biblioteca Nueva; 1945. p. 59.

320 Feijóo, S. The Wisdom of Juan Without Anything: Signs in the Expression of the People. Sayings. Santa Clara, Cuba: Signos Magazine. No. 14, Year 5, No. 2; January-April 1974. p. 199.

~~~